LORD, SAVE ME FROM ME!

GEORGE DAVIS

LORD, SAVE ME FROM ME!
Copyright © 2008 by George Davis

ISBN: 0-9793192-8-5
978-0-9793192-8-0

Published by

LIFEBRIDGE
B O O K S
P.O. BOX 49428
CHARLOTTE, NC 28277

Printed in the United States of America.

CONTENTS

FOREWORD

In this book, *Lord Save Me from Me!*, my friend, George Davis invites us to confront our own personal issues—conflict within ourselves. Bishop Davis uses sound biblical principals to ensure we have victory over adversity. We should always be prepared for spiritual warfare in whatever form it may come. Yet, are we equipped to handle self encounter? No one knows us like we know ourselves. In this powerful book you will learn how to handle some surprising and not so surprising enemies within while building a stronger relationship with God the Father.

We are God's most precious creation and He has provided all we need to battle any situation. Bishop Davis has done an exceptional job in capturing godly principles to be used in the rescue of ourselves from ourselves.

— Marilyn Hickey, Minister, Co-founder of Orchard Road Christian Center, Englewood, CO

We often go through life making the same mistakes and finding ourselves failing in the same areas over and over again. We often blame Satan, our past, and any other convenient scapegoat. In his latest book, *Lord, Save Me from Me!*, George Davis uncovers the true fact that the real enemy lies within. We are, at most times, our own worst enemy. Satan is certainly behind it all, but we play well into his hands.

Taken straight from the Bible, this book contains revelation knowledge regarding the what, where, when, and why we always face the same issues in life. Most importantly, it breaks down God's prescription for how we are to respond and conduct ourselves throughout this learning process. We are not to condemn ourselves, but rather, we are to learn from our mistakes and allow God to show us the way of escape that He has provided for us.

While you may be, at this moment, your own worst enemy, George Davis shows you how to come out of the rut you are in and find the pathway to peace within yourself. *Lord Save Me from Me!* will teach you how to face your fears, how to use simple biblical tools that will equip and help you get through your challenges. Learn how to "Let go and Let God."

The Lord never intended for man to go through life's difficulties alone. In His Word, He promises never to leave nor forsake us. You will truly be blessed by this book. *Lord Save Me from Me!* is a book you should include in your Christian living library.

– Bishop Keith A. Butler, Founder and Pastor, Word of Faith International Christian Center, Southfield, MI

INTRODUCTION

Let me begin by asking you a few questions:

- Are you satisfied with the level of spiritual growth you have obtained up to this point and content to just cruise along in life, looking forward to the great "by and by"?
- Do you want out of the rut in your marriage?
- Do you desire a better relationship with your children and a deeper walk with God?
- Do you long to receive everything God has ordained for you through the shed blood of Jesus?

Then this book is for you! If you will embrace the spiritual truths on these pages and apply them, they will take you to higher heights, and deeper depths. This information will revolutionize your entire life!

Contrary to popular belief, especially among Christians, the biggest hindrance to our walking in God's best is not other people, "the system," or the devil. We often spend time pointing our finger at others, praying and asking God to deliver us from bad marriages and other relationships, jobs, and Satan's traps. Many times husbands will say, "Lord, just fix my wife." Likewise, wives will spend time asking God to fix their husbands. When in reality, Jesus has taken care of all our challenges and the devil over 2000 years ago.

The Bible declares, *"For this purpose, the Son of God was*

manifest to destroy the works of the evil one" (1 John 3:8).

So, the devil isn't even our problem. Therefore, the one thing that keeps us from doing all God has ordained for us to do is our own selves. When we obey only *part* of His Word, we become complacent in our Christian journey and refuse to allow the Lord to help us mature in Him. We stunt our own spiritual growth when we prevent ourselves from moving forward in the things of God.

AN INSIDE WORK

I have come to a place in my Christian walk where I realize that if I am going to reach the highest heights and carry out everything God has ordained for my life, I will have to stop looking at what is happening on the outside and say, "Lord, I know that if I just allow You to work on the inside, there is no devil in hell that can keep me down, nor any system that can hold me back."

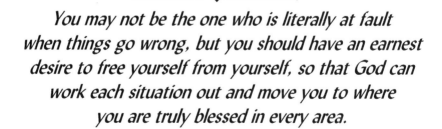

You may not be the one who is literally at fault when things go wrong, but you should have an earnest desire to free yourself from yourself, so that God can work each situation out and move you to where you are truly blessed in every area.

Second Timothy 2:23-24 in the Amplified version of the Bible reads, *"But refuse (shut your mind against, have nothing to do with) trifling (ill-informed, unedifying, stupid) controversies over ignorant questionings, for you know that they foster strife and breed quarrel. And the servant of the Lord must not be quarrelsome (fighting and contending). Instead, he must be kindly to everyone and mild-tempered [preserving the bond of peace]; he must be a skilled and suitable teacher, patient and forbearing and willing to suffer wrong."*

Notice, God's Word says that part of your role as a leader is to instruct those who oppose themselves. People can be against what is really best for their lives and become their own worst enemy. We can unknowingly be the source of our own pain and cause ourselves to keep circling in the same wilderness without ever making it to our Promised Land.

Sadly, we usually end up pointing the finger at our job, church, spouse, or children, complaining, "Well, if this person, place or thing would just change then I would be fine." Yet, the Bible teaches that it is quite possible for us to be in a position where we are opposing or hurting ourselves.

The Scripture continues, *"He must correct his opponents with courtesy and gentleness, in the hope that God may grant that they will repent and come to know the Truth [that they will perceive and recognize and become accurately acquainted with and acknowledge it], and that they may come to their senses [and] escape out of the snare of the devil, having been held captive by him, [henceforth] to do His [God's] will"* (verses 25-26 AMP).

The phrase "come to their senses" is from the Greek word *ananepho* which is translated "recover"—literally meaning to become sober or regain one's senses. God is clearly saying it is possible for a believer to be against himself. If you find yourself in such a position, you need to depend on God to help you recover and get *you* to a place where you are sober again.

YOUR OWN WORST ENEMY?

Anyone who understands anything about alcohol knows that if a person is drunk, you can't just snap your fingers and make them instantly sober. There is a process involved. Often we end up doing the wrong thing and making bad decisions because we allow our flesh to dictate our actions instead of being led by the Spirit. God desires to help us reach a level where we are no longer fighting against ourselves or being our own worst enemy. Instead, the Lord wants us to sober up and be alert so we can clearly see His direction for every area of our lives.

Scripture tells us, *"Therefore if any man be in Christ, he is a new creature: old things are passed away; behold, all things are become new"* (2 Corinthians 5:17). The Amplified Bible says, *"...Behold, the fresh and new has come!"*

The flesh does not become reborn once a person is born again. If you were 5 feet 9 inches tall before you got saved, you will still be 5 feet 9 inches tall after your salvation. If you weighed 150 pounds before, you will still weigh 150 pounds after. So, nothing changes physically when a person is saved. Yet the Scripture states, *"...behold all things are become new."*

When a person accepts Jesus Christ as his Lord and Savior, on the inside, he spiritually becomes a brand new person.

THE REAL YOU

Man is a tri-part being. He is a spirit being who possesses a soul, which consists of his mind, will, and emotions. The spirit man lives in a physical body. The house of flesh and bones you are walking around in is not the real you, nor is your soul. The real you is that person on the inside, that spirit being which identifies with God.

When you are born again, you become a new creation in Christ Jesus. You may look and feel the same—and you may even retain some of your former ways of thinking or a few old habits still trying to cling to you. However, when you make the confession of faith and declare Jesus Christ to be Lord over your life, the Bible says that on the inside of you, the fresh and new has been birthed.

———— ❖ ————

You don't just drive through a spiritual car wash, and get cleaned up so you just look a little sharper on the outside and feel better.

You literally experience the greatest miracle that could ever happen: you become a completely different person who has never existed before! That old, dead spirit is evicted and a brand new spirit, made in the very image and likeness of God, comes to take residence in your body.

From that point forward, on the inside you look just like God. Your nature is just like His. Why? Because the person living within has been transformed—even if your flesh remains the same.

FACING THE CONFLICT

Let's say you are thirty-five when you are born again. The past fifteen years or so, your body has become accustomed to frequenting certain places on Friday nights and for many years your body has been used to receiving sexual gratification. Just because you were saved last Sunday does not mean those desires will leave your body automatically. Your flesh still feels obligated to appease itself.

For fifteen years you have been thinking one way, getting out of jams on your own, utilizing the philosophy of the streets or what you learned in the high school locker room. Well, when you became born again your emotions did not necessarily get saved. You have the same feelings you had before your born again experience. They may cause you to cry as soon as something challenging arises, or

11

they may move you to get upset, lose control, and curse at people when you feel they have wronged you.

Let's face it, you have been acting this way for fifteen years —letting your emotions run rampant, free to do whatever they please—but now that you are a new creation in Christ you have a desire to react and do things God's way. So, there is a tug of war. *You must teach the "real you" on the inside how to dominate the "old you" that has been running the show for so long.*

How is this transformation possible? Keep reading.

ONE

THE BATTLE WITHIN

There is an unseen conflict taking place on the inside of you every single day of your life. Yes, right now while you are reading this book, there is a battle being waged—a war between good and evil.

The real you, your spirit man, is all good. Yet, in your flesh, your emotions and your un-renewed mind, there are still old habits that are trying to dominate you *and pull you back into hell.* Long-held tendencies such as moodiness, losing your temper, and gossiping try to ensnare you. While the real you on the inside is screaming, "I am not like that anymore. Lord, please save me from me!"

We need to understand that in order to ever be saved from ourselves we must first acknowledge that this battle exists. Let us see how the apostle Paul describes it in Romans 7:15-25. The Amplified Bible reads:

> *For I do not understand my own actions [I am baffled, bewildered]. I do not practice or accomplish what I wish, but I do the very thing that I loathe [which my moral instinct condemns]. Now if I do [habitually] what is contrary to my desire, [that means that] I acknowledge and agree that the Law is good (morally excellent) and that I take sides with it.*

However, it is no longer I who do the deed, but the sin [principle] which is at home in me and has possession of me. For I know that nothing good dwells within me, that is, in my flesh. I can will what is right, but I cannot perform it. [I have the intention and urge to do what is right, but no power to carry it out.] For I fail to practice the good deeds I desire to do, but the evil deeds that I do not desire to do are what I am [ever] doing.

Now if I do what I do not desire to do, it is no longer I doing it [it is not myself that acts], but the sin [principle] which dwells within me [fixed and operating in my soul]. So I find it to be a law (a rule of action of my being) that when I want to do what is right and good, evil is ever present with me and I am subject to its insistent demands. For I endorse and delight in the Law of God in my inmost self [with my new nature]. But I discern in my bodily members [in the sensitive appetites and wills of the flesh] a different law (rule of action) at war against the law of my mind (my reason) and making me a prisoner to the law of sin that dwells in my bodily organs [in the sensitive appetites and wills of the flesh].

Oh unhappy, and pitiable and wretched man that I am! Who will release and deliver me from [the shackles of] this body of death? Oh thank God! [He will!] through Jesus Christ (the Anointed One) our Lord! So then indeed I, of myself with the mind and heart, serve the law of God, but with the flesh the law of sin.

The Message Bible explains it this way:

I can anticipate the response that is coming: 'I know that

14

all God's commands are spiritual but I am not. Isn't this also your experience?' Yes. I am full of myself—after all, I've spent a long time in sin's prison. What I don't understand about myself is that I decide one way, but then I act another, doing things I absolutely despise. So if I can't be trusted to figure out what is best for myself and then do it, it becomes obvious that God's command is necessary. But I need something more!

For if I know the law but still can't keep it, and if the power of sin within me keeps sabotaging my best intentions, I obviously need help! I realize that I don't have what it takes. I can will it, but I can't do it. I decide to do good, but I don't really do it; I decide not to do bad, but then I do it anyway. My decisions, such as they are, don't result in actions. Something has gone wrong deep within me and gets the better of me every time. It happens so regularly that it is predictable. The moment I decide to do good, sin is there to trip me up. I truly delight in God's commands, but it's pretty obvious that not all of me joins in that delight. Parts of me covertly rebel, and just when I least expect it, they take charge.

I've tried everything and nothing helps. I'm at the end of my rope. Is there no one who can do anything for me? Isn't that the real question? The answer, thank God, is that Jesus Christ can and does. He acted to set things right in this life of contradictions where I want to serve God with all my heart and mind, but am pulled by the influence of sin to do something totally different (Romans 7:15-25).

I believe this perfectly describes the war that is raging on the inside of us all. I'm not just referring to sins such as fornicating or committing adultery. I am talking about when you have decided once and for all that you are no longer going to sit around with an attitude, yet still end up with that same foul mental outlook. For example, when you have vowed you are never again going to get yourself trapped in debt. Then six months later, you find yourself chained in the same financial prison.

A MENTAL TRANSFORMATION

Why is it we want to do what's right on the inside, but in our flesh, we end up in such a struggle that it becomes a major challenge? The answer is simple. In our spirit man, we always want to do exactly what the Almighty says, but in order for us to be able to carry it out, there must be a process of consistently and continually renewing the mind.

God's Word teaches: *"Be not conformed to this world: but be ye transformed by the renewing of your mind"* (Romans 12:2). Once you are born again there is nothing inwardly that resembles the world. If I could split you open, and let your spirit be the only thing visible, you would say, "Man, I don't look anything like the world—or even have the same appetites."

Your flesh man, your unrenewed mind, however, still has the tendency and desire to drift toward the attractions of the world. It wants to hear and watch all the things society listens to and craves. The Bible calls for a drastic change—by the renewing of our thinking.

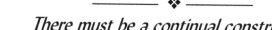

There must be a continual construction project, a major ongoing renovation taking place in your thought life every day.

16

In order for our actions to change, a "mental transformation" must take place. The process will begin when we start attending a church where the Word of God is being taught on a weekly basis. For instance, suppose you are feeling "a little achy" in your body. Formerly, you would make a mad dash for the medicine cabinet, trying to gulp down all the Alka Seltzer Plus® or Vicks Nyquil® you can get your hands on, thinking, "Oh, I feel so sick; I must be catching the flu!"

Now, the first thing that comes to your mind is, "Wait a minute, Jesus Himself, took my infirmities and bore my sickness and with His stripes I was healed (1 Peter 2:24). Therefore body, I refuse to let you give into this sickness." This type of response is evidence of your mind being renewed or changed by the Word of God.

THE REMODELING PROJECT

We were recently involved in a renovation project on the second floor of one of our church buildings. When the contractors arrived to begin the work, they didn't just walk in and start putting up wall boards. First, they ordered a dumpster and then waited for delivery. Why did they need a dumpster? Because there were materials that had to be ripped out and removed from the building before the renovation could go forward.

During the process, people commented on how wonderful the building looked compared to what it was in the past. However, there was one area that still wasn't completed—and no one saw the inside because it wasn't open to the general public. From the outside it seemed finished, but if you took a peak inside it looked a wreck.

The same thing is true for many believers. When they are converted and God begins a divine construction on them, He starts

17

changing various areas of their lives. When they come to church they look fine, are all dressed up, and know the right words to say. If the pastor encourages, "Lift your hands and say Hallelujah," they respond, "Hallelujah!" They know the right time to stand up and exactly when to sit down. But they are not willing to admit there is still some hidden "stuff" lingering on the inside in some unfinished rooms.

These areas may not be exposed for all to see, but they are still in desperate need of renovation. From the outside, everything appears wonderful. They are able to make it through another church service without anyone being the wiser. Then they go home feeling relieved because they can finally relax from all the hard work and effort it took to put up a good front!

Does this sound familiar? If it does, then the time has come to clean house—to remove the skeletons from the closet and open up those rooms where we have not allowed God to have access. When we make this decision, there will be no more entering the sanctuary with a good-looking exterior, yet inwardly being all torn up.

So pull up to the "Holy Ghost dumpster," we are going to dig deep and start remodeling!

TWO

PULLING DOWN STRONGHOLDS

Many ask, "Why are there some aspects of our lives that change right away while others appear to be more stubborn, taking longer for us to yield those hidden parts to God?"

The apostle Paul gave the answer in writing to the believers at Corinth: *"For though we walk in the flesh, we do not war after the flesh: (For the weapons of our warfare are not carnal, but mighty through God to the pulling down of strongholds;)"* (2 Corinthians 10:3-4).

The word *stronghold* in the Greek literally means "castle." The New American Standard Bible says, *"For the weapons of our warfare are not of flesh, but divinely powerful for the destruction of fortresses."*

Another definition I use for *stronghold* is "a demonically-induced pattern of thinking." It is where the devil has so programmed a person's mind that he automatically thinks a certain way. He has been doing this for so long that he has worn a groove in his thought processes.

WELL-WORN PATHS

When I was growing up in Detroit, there was an open field across the street from my cousin's house. We didn't have a baseball diamond to play on, so we would go to this big grassy area and play ball. We made our own home plate. There was a tree off to one side that we identified as first base. We would find an old hubcap or whatever was available and make it second base. We had a spot where a parking meter had been knocked over; that was third base. If you made it back to home plate, you were coming back to where you started.

In the summer, we played baseball every day from sun up to sun down for so long in that field that you could see a path had been worn in the grass. It did not matter how much it rained or how much sunlight it received. That worn out path showed you the direction we ran from home plate to third base. We just kept running in the same spot over and over.

This is exactly what a stronghold is. It is repetitive thinking that has been in your life for so long it has worn a path in your thought process. When God steps in, He can clean up everything else around, yet never touch that area—unless you permit Him to.

CAN WE BREAK FREE?

Each of us has strongholds. Depending upon your background, yours may be different from someone else's, but we all have issues in our lives that require God's help if we are to ever break free.

Let me give you some examples.

A stronghold could be a lack of discipline. You may have read best selling books and listened to numerous tapes on the topic. You have bought a Franklin Planner®, a Day Runner®, an organizer, a pager, a tape recorder, and a Palm Pilot®; yet with all these combined, you remain undisciplined. You still miss appointments and arrive late for work, church, and meetings.

Poor eating habits can be a stronghold. The first of every year, you commit to losing ten pounds. For the first two months you lose five—half of your goal. Then comes March, and those pounds are just like that old song with the words, "I was lost, but now I am found."

It is not because you failed to follow the diet's instructions properly. The reason it didn't work is because you have a stronghold of poor eating habits. Unless you break free from what has you firmly in its grip, you can try every weight loss program on the market and none of them will work. You can say you are not going to eat anything except crackers, but those pounds will find you again if you do not do something about the powerful hold of poor eating habits.

Lust can be a stronghold, and many Christians are bound by this. They will never tell anybody because they are embarrassed about this carnal craving.

———— ❖ ————

What is the answer? We must reach the place
where we can come to the house of God, own up
to our strongholds and receive help.

A believer should be able to confide and say to another believer, "Look, I am having a challenge in this area and my flesh is getting the best of me."

FACING THE CHALLENGE

In far too many cases we have created a pride-filled environment within the church. As a result we have immature Christians who end up "shooting" their brother or sister when they are down instead of extending a hand and helping them get back on their feet.

Every week there are people who come to church and are hurting deeply. Your brother does not want to keep watching that pornographic filth. He does not want to keep going to that obscene website. He knows he should not keep picking up that magazine he promised himself and God he would not look at again. He is having a struggle, and he does not have anyone to confide in or pray with. It is going to take us, as the Body of Christ, to stop walking around in a religious bubble—just showing up at church on Sunday, acting as if everything is picture perfect.

There is nothing wrong with you just because you are having trouble in a particular area. There may be an issue you are dealing with, but that person sitting next to you in church is struggling with his or her own problems. They just don't want to tell you.

The power comes when we reach the place where we have a godly person in our lives whom we have enough trust in to go to and confess, "I am having a challenge with this. I need you to pray with me. I need to be accountable to you."

THE PROBLEM OF REBELLION

You do not have to suffer the rest of your days walking around the same mountain. Almighty God can help set you free. Some of the problem is the devil trying to take advantage, but most of it is that you have not really made a total decision to change.

Selfishness, inconsistency, and rebellion to authority can all be strongholds. The reason many people keep changing jobs, or have moved to eight churches in two years, it is not because there is anything wrong with the job or the church. They keep bouncing all over the place because of a problem with rebellion.

There may be times the Lord will require you to serve under a person who may seem hard to deal with, but they can help you subdue that rebellious nature in your flesh. If you harbor rebellion in your heart toward natural leadership, you will also have the same resistance toward God's leading.

Occasionally, it is necessary to have a person tell you to do something which is exactly opposite of what you desire in the natural. The last thing your flesh needs is for somebody to constantly agree with you and say "Yes" to you all the time.

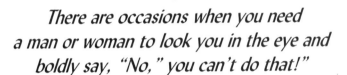

There are occasions when you need a man or woman to look you in the eye and boldly say, "No," you can't do that!"

When this happens, go ahead and allow your flesh to go screaming into the bedroom and let it cry, stomp, spit, or whatever it's going to do. When the urge returns, you still must say, "Self, you are not doing it!"

In some cases, the very thing hindering you from reaching the next level with God is your hesitancy to discipline your flesh. Just say, "Yes, Lord!" Be obedient and willing to take direction His way.

The reason some individuals want to be an evangelist, is that they despise the thought of being accountable. Any evangelist who is just doing his or her own ministry and is not submitted to a pastor is out of the will of God.

From personal experience I can tell you that everybody needs a pastor. Not only am I a minister to a congregation, but I *have* a pastor. If I pick up the phone and share with him a plan that the

Spirit of God has been revealing to me, he may begin to give me words of wisdom I may not have considered. You'd better believe I am going to pay close attention to what he has to say.

I am convinced the reason the Lord can trust me and take me to higher levels is because I have purposed in my heart to be submissive to authority.

"GET REAL!"

Here are several other dangerous strongholds:

- Being easily offended—where your feelings are always getting hurt
- Having low self-esteem or a low self-image
- Being constantly negative
- Walking around filled with insecurities
- Procrastination and lack of organization
- Instability, murmuring, complaining, and lying
- Stealing, unfaithfulness, and having a bad attitude
- Lack of commitment, pride, gossiping, and meddling in other people's business
- Anger, greed, laziness, and lack of time-lines

There are certain individuals who, no matter what the occasion, are always late. You can move the time back thirty minutes and they still do not arrive at the desired place on schedule. You may ride with a person who has their clock set forty-five minutes ahead—and they are still tardy. But according to their "mental clock" they are well within time. That, my friend, is a stronghold.

The Bible tells us, *"Neither is there any creature that is not manifest in his sight: but all things are naked and opened unto the eyes of him with whom we have to do"* (Hebrews 4:13).

God knows everything. Even when we are not honest with ourselves, He still knows. In order for the Lord to be able to help save us from ourselves, one of the first steps we must take is to be "real" with Him.

There are many walking around with "wax"—or a false face—on. We have been putting on an act for so long that even when we get into our prayer time with God we begin telling Him the same lies we tell everybody else. I believe the Almighty in heaven is telling us, "Get real! I know what you were thinking. Get rid of the wax. Lay that stronghold down at My altar, and let Me help you with it once and for all."

TIME TO DIG DEEPER

There were things in my life God totally freed me from, and they will never touch me again. Yet, I'm not perfect. There are certain areas I still have to deal with. However, over time, I plan to be able to say they are no longer an issue for me. This is because I have made a commitment to open up and allow God to heal and repair what is necessary. As Scripture counsels, *"Wherefore gird up the loins of your mind, be sober, and hope to the end for the grace that is to be brought unto you at the revelation of Jesus Christ"* (1 Peter 1:13). The New International Version of the Bible reads, *"Therefore, prepare your minds for action."*

———— ❖ ————

The phrase "gird up the loins of you mind" literally means "get ready to do something difficult."

If you think what you are learning right now and what you will discover in the rest of this book is going to be easy, you are in for

25

a shock. I am not talking about the minor surface issues you have been working on. Rather, it concerns digging deeper and dealing with the behaviors and actions you don't even realize you are doing.

It is not going to be a walk in the park. I wish I could just give you a positive confession and say, "This is going to be the easiest thing in the world." The truth is, you'd better be ready for a fight.

Your flesh is not going to want to relinquish what it has been so used to doing. Your emotions are not going to like giving up responding as they have always responded. Your thoughts are going to wrestle with you. This is why the Word of God tells us to gird up the loins of your mind.

WHO'S IN CONTROL?

Get ready to do what is beyond your own ability—and prepare your mind for action. Jesus says, "*I am the vine, ye are the branches: He that abideth in me, and I in him, the same bringeth forth much fruit: for without me ye can do nothing*" (John 15:5).

If you don't give Christ Lordship over every corner of your being it will eventually destroy you. If you attempt to personally take control and think, "I am through with letting Jesus handle things. Thank You, Lord, but I think I can take over from here"—your life will end up in shambles.

Anytime we attempt to take charge of our own future, it leads to destruction. Jesus is still declaring, "Apart from me, you can do nothing."

When you reach the level where you can be truthful with both God and yourself, He is able to help you. The Lord is tired of seeing you distressed and hurting. He needs you to partner with Him and allow Him fix the problem and repair your life.

Are you ready for His divine assistance?

THREE

ANOINTED THOUGHTS

I cannot overemphasize the fact that if our actions are going to be different, a change must take place in our thinking. As Paul tells us, *"For who has known the mind of the Lord, that he may instruct him? But we have the mind of Christ"* (1 Corinthians 2:16).

Notice the Scripture says we *have* the mind of Christ. The word *Christ* is not Jesus' last name. *Christ* means "the Anointed One, and His Anointing."

So when we say we have the mind of Christ, we are literally declaring there is an anointing on our thinking. And in order for this to occur, we must consistently have anointed thoughts.

Where do these come from? God's anointed Word. Thus, having the mind of Christ is truly having our thinking flooded with Scripture instead of being saturated with the ways of Satan and the world.

If I were writing the above verse about myself, I would probably say I am *getting* the mind of Christ. I have a whole lot of thoughts that are in line with God's Word, but I will admit there are times some of my thinking is not all that anointed. But God assures us we *have* the mind of Christ—it is ours! You see, the Lord always speaks to us in terms of where He sees our destiny, not where we are right now.

The Bible says that by the stripes of Jesus we *were* healed. This means we are made whole even if we have symptoms in our body right now. This is why we need to exercise our faith and make adjustments in our lifestyle to lay claim to what God promises already belongs to us.

Scripture declares we are a prosperous people, so we need to start living as such.

God's Word teaches that Jesus has given us His peace. This is a spiritual truth, but from a natural standpoint you may have chaos erupting in your life. If so, it is necessary to use your faith and make the necessary corrections until your natural world begins to line up with the spiritual truths which declare you have peace and rest.

MAKE THE ADJUSTMENTS

Back to the mind of Christ, according to the Word and as a believer, you have His mind at this very moment. However, if you harbor thoughts, attitudes and ways of thinking that are not in tune with God's Word, you are out of step with the Father. This doesn't happen automatically. In order for you to actually walk in this truth, you have to access the mind of Christ by saying, "Yes I agree with it by faith"—just as you do for healing, prosperity, and peace. Then you must continue to make whatever adjustments are needed until the natural fact begins to mirror the spiritual truth that declares your thought patterns are anointed.

It's a biblical principle that as a man thinketh in his heart, so is he (Proverbs 23:7). If I am thinking a certain way, eventually I am going to act on that thought and it will become who I am. If I want to be transformed into a man or woman who is walking in God's fullness, then I have to make sure that my thoughts become anointed.

28

CAST IT DOWN!

What are Spirit-inspired, anointed thoughts? They are ones that agree with the Bible. When God's Word declares you are healed, but you have a fear of dying of cancer, a heaven-blessed thought needs to replace the image of dying. Once more, you need to stand on what the Bible promises—that by the stripes of Jesus you were healed (1 Peter 2:24).

———— ❖ ————

Our mandate is to take every non-anointed
thought that penetrates our mind and arrest it.

We accomplish this by apprehending any evil thought which enters our thinking and replacing it with what God approves. After the Bible tells us we are to pull down strongholds, it speaks of *"Casting down imaginations, and every high thing that exalteth itself against the knowledge of God, and bringing into captivity every thought to the obedience of Christ; And having in a readiness to revenge all disobedience, when your obedience is fulfilled"* (2 Corinthians 10:5-6).

In essence, we are to crush every concept or idea which is contrary to the Word of God.

TAKE AUTHORITY

Perhaps you are one who has dealt with insecurity all of your life. You have felt people don't like you or that you fail to measure up to the standards of others. You may be saying, "Wow, so-and-so can sing; or he is so smart; or the Lord is really using her." But the Bible declares that God has made us righteous—which includes you!

Instead of sitting back and allowing the idea that you don't

29

measure up to dwell in your mind, cast it down, because God also paid for it with Jesus' blood. That carnal thought has exalted itself against the Father's knowledge. The negative image is attempting to become higher in your mind than God's Word. Therefore, this thought is not anointed.

Both good and bad have a right to hang around in your thinking if you let them, because the mind is the battlefield—and your thoughts determine whether you win or lose.

Here is the bottom line: you have authority over your mind; it belongs to you, not the other way around. You can control what thoughts enter your head. The Bible says, "Casting down imaginations," so you have to defeat the thought and disable its power. You can't just declare, "I cast that thought down and I bind it." That's just half of the equation. The other half is replacing the negative with what is anointed.

"Having in a readiness to revenge all disobedience" (2 Corinthians 10:6) means you must protect and keep guard over your mind. You need to be expecting that Satan will send bad thoughts, especially in the areas in which you have been challenged. Remember, the devil will try his best to keep you from doing things God's way. Every time he tempts you with a wicked thought, you have to cast it down and replace it! When Satan tells you to get on your computer and click to a pornographic website, you have to declare the words of David: "*I will set no wicked thing before mine eyes*" (Psalm 101:3).

Such thoughts may cross your mind two hundred times in a day, and two hundred times you will have to cast them down and find a replacement. When you become developed in the area of casting down non-anointed thoughts and replacing them with what God anoints, you'll find that as time goes on those ideas from Satan will be fewer and fewer until eventually you are no longer challenged in that area. However, you will still need to keep up your guard.

DISCIPLINE YOUR THINKING

In order for us to manifest the mind of the Anointed One, we have to develop a system whereby we purposefully deal with every evil thought that pops up in our thinking. Many people, in error, believe that nothing can be done about these mental images. And until they begin to seriously work on the matter, their thought lives will remain undisciplined, allowing their minds to wander and think on things they have no business considering.

———— ❖ ————

We cannot let our minds drift aimlessly and allow the devil to deposit thoughts that really aren't our own.

Please understand, Satan is not all knowing; neither is he omnipresent—meaning he can't be everywhere at the same time. There is only one devil, but he has an army of imps, wimps, and demons helping him. But since he does not know everything, he has no idea what is going on inside your heart. His trick is to attempt to drop a thought in your mind to find out how you will respond. He will watch your reactions. This is why we as believers have to be strong and discipline our thinking.

MIND-CASTLES

Be honest with yourself. In order to change what is taking place in your mind, you have to admit those thoughts exist so you can deal with them and do what the Bible says regarding their removal. Do you think God would tell you to arrest and capture every thought if you didn't have the ability and the power to do so? Of course, not.

Low self-esteem starts with a single thought. It may have been planted from the time you were a child. Over the years, all those ideas and concepts of what you could and couldn't do have built a castle in your mind. Later, when God speaks to your heart and begins to tell you His vision for your future, if you're not careful, that castle of low self-esteem will immediately start sowing thoughts that say you can't accomplish what God is calling you to do. So, you have to bind and take prisoner of the thought by saying, "No, that is not anointed! I break its power. It will not linger in my mind. I cast you down and replace you with the Word of God. I claim the promise that I can do all things through Christ, which strengthens me."

Therefore, if I don't feel like I can succeed, I agree with heaven. I place God's Words in my mind and my mouth and I command the devil to stop his aggression against me!

Don't make such a commitment just once. Declare it daily—as often as those thoughts arise. Paraphrase 2 Corinthians 10:6 and say, "I am going to have a readiness to revenge all disobedience."

ON GUARD!

When I was growing up, my stepfather was in the military and was stationed at Fort Louis in Washington. I remember so clearly that every time we went on base there were always armed guards stationed all around. Every car that approached was stopped and checked to make sure it was supposed to be there. That would make perfect sense to me if we were at war, but in times of peace, when there was nothing unforseen going on, the guards were still at their post.

There was never a time we pulled up to the base and discovered that the security had taken the day off. Whether it was early in the morning or late at night, there were always armed soldiers checking every vehicle that entered.

The Bible says we must be on "readiness"—having our minds on guard, screening every thought that tries to break through. If you wake up from a dream at 4:00 A.M., screen those thoughts and check them in. If it is lunchtime and Satan's ideas begin trying to show up, do the same.

Teach both your physical and spiritual system that your thought reservoir will not become a garbage dump for all kinds of stray thoughts to linger.

———— ❖ ————

Keep reminding yourself that your mind is the battlefield, and whoever wins the conflict over your thoughts wins the battle over your life.

Jesus taught, *"If any man has ears to hear, let him hear. And he said unto them, Take heed what you hear"* (Mark 4: 23-24). The NIV translates the words, *"Consider carefully what you hear."*

In order to control non-anointed thoughts, you must take authority over what you put in front of your eyes, and what you allow yourself to hear. Your eye and ear gates are the birthing center for thoughts.

TAKE CHARGE

Right not, let me ask you to think with me about a tiny malnourished baby girl in Darfur. The reason you weren't considering that child ten minutes ago is because I had not called your attention to her.

On the other hand, picture yourself living in a three million dollar mansion with two luxury cars, a maid, a butler, and a large room that you can dedicate as a prayer closet! Why weren't you thinking about your estate prior to this moment? Because you were not yet presented with the image or information.

Consequently, if you are going to control non-anointed thoughts, you have to start taking charge of every sight and sound.

———— ❖ ————

Don't allow the devil to have access to
your thinking patterns. It is hard for you to
tear down a castle while it is being built.

The key to taking charge is found in Mark 7:5: *"Then the Pharisees and scribes asked him, Why walk not thy disciples according to the traditions of the elders, but eat bread with unwashen hands?"*

The religious elders were asking Jesus why His disciples did not follow the traditions and go through the full ceremonial washing and cleansing before they ate? Notice Jesus' response in verses 14-19:

And when he had called all the people unto him, he said unto them, Hearken unto me every one of you, and understand: There is nothing from without a man [or outside of a man], that entering into him can defile him: but the things which come out of him, those are they that defile the man. If any man have ears to hear, let him hear. And when he was entered into the house from the people, his disciples

34

*asked him concerning the parable. And he saith unto them,
Are ye so without understanding also? Do ye not perceive,
that whatsoever thing from without entereth into the man it
can not defile him; Because it entereth not into his heart, but
into the belly, and goeth out into the draught, purging all
meats.*

Jesus was saying if a person just eats and does not wash their
hands, it may not be the most hygienic thing in the world, but it is
not going to defile him. Whatever you eat goes into your stomach
and is not the composition of who you really are. He continued,
*"That which cometh out of a man, that defileth the man. For from
within, out of the heart of men, proceed evil thoughts"* (verse 20).

THE SOURCE OF WICKED THINKING

The words of the Bible are anointed, but not necessarily the
punctuation. It may have been added by the translators in an
attempt to make the passage easier to read. Most of the time they
did a terrific job, but every now and then you'll find punctuation
that, in my opinion, is a little bit off. For example, Mark 7:21 reads,
*"For from within, out of the heart of men, proceed evil thoughts,
adulteries..."*

If you think about what Jesus is saying here—keeping it in the
context of this teaching—a colon should be placed after the word
"thoughts" instead of a comma. He's not implying that adultery
comes from within a man, but thoughts of adultery do: *"...from
within, out of the heart of men, proceed evil thoughts: adulteries..."*

Then Jesus goes on to list the types of evil thoughts that could
flow out of a man. What kind? Thoughts of adultery, fornication,

35

murder, stealing, covetousness, wickedness, deceitfulness, lascivious-
ness or having no control, an evil eye, thoughts of blasphemy, of
pride and of foolishness (Mark 7:21-22).

Jesus continues, *"All these evil things come from within, and
defile the man"* (verse 23), He is telling us:

- Before a person acts out in pride, the *thought* of pride
  comes first.
- Before a person ever carries out an act of fornication, the
  thought was already there.
- Before a person ever commits the act of stealing, it all
  begins with a *thought.*

DECLARE YOUR DESTINY

If any of these have been areas in your life which have been hard
to overcome, you can't afford to wait until the action is ready to
manifest itself before doing something about it. You have to collar
that desire when it is still in the infantile stage of being an initial
thought. Scripture gives this example:

> *And when Simon saw that through laying on of the
> apostles' hands the Holy Ghost was given, he offered them
> money, Saying, Give me also this power, that on
> whomsoever I lay hands, he may receive the Holy Ghost. But
> Peter said unto him, Thy money perish with thee, because
> thou hast thought that the gift of God may be purchased
> with money. Thou hast neither part nor lot in this matter: for
> thy heart is not right in the sight of God. Repent therefore
> of this thy wickedness, and pray God, if perhaps the thought
> of thine heart may be forgiven thee* (Acts 8:18-22).

Peter tells him the thought that arose in his heart needs to be dealt with. He counseled Simon not just to pray and ask God's forgiveness for what he had done, but to go back and ask the Lord to help him deal with the evil thought that gave birth to the action.

I tell myself on a daily basis that I am an anointed man of God. I don't care if anyone else believes it; I do! My belief that there is an anointing on my life is not based on how many people show up for church each week or on how many CD's or books are purchased. My assurance that there is an anointing on me is founded on what I see in the Word of God, and what the Lord has confirmed in my heart. Therefore—on purpose—I declare out of my mouth every time I get ready to minister, "There is an anointing on my life that will change the lives of people."

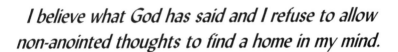

I believe what God has said and I refuse to allow non-anointed thoughts to find a home in my mind.

I declare and prophesy my own destiny. As a result, with God's help, I end up creating my own world and walk in an anointing. Therefore, because I believe and say it, this begins to come to pass.

WHO IS PROMPTING?

Thoughts played a role in the betrayal of Jesus. The Bible records, *"Now before the feast of the passover, when Jesus knew that his hour was come that he should depart out of this world unto the Father, having loved his own which were in the world, he loved them unto the end. And supper being ended, the devil having now put into the heart of Judas Iscariot, Simon's son, to betray him"*

37

(John 13:1-2). The NIV translates it, *"the devil had already prompted"* him.

This is literally saying that Satan had placed the thought of betrayal in the heart of Judas. From where did his act of disloyalty spring? It was the result of a non-anointed thought Judas allowed to fester without dealing with the matter. He accepted it, acted upon it, and this destroyed his whole life.

That was not Judas' thought—he had no personal desire to betray Jesus. However, he allowed the devil to prompt him without dealing with the issue.

This happens to people constantly. A husband and wife can be getting along very well in their marriage, then all of the sudden they have a disagreement. The devil prompts one of them with an implanted thought suggesting, "Someone else would take better care of you than she does." He will whisper to the woman, "You married him, and all he ever does is go off and hang out with his friends. You are always left sitting here with no one to talk to. That guy at the office would sure enjoy your company."

I want to help you recognize where all this begins. Sir, you don't just one day walk out of your home, commit adultery on your spouse, break up your marriage and have your wife and children leave you. It all starts with a mental process. For this reason you must make a decision that when thoughts penetrate your mind that do not line up with the Bible, you will refuse to let them take root.

"WHAT IF?"

Please pay attention to what Jesus said regarding what takes place in your mind and heart: *"And as they thus spake, Jesus himself stood in the midst of them, and saith unto them, Peace be unto you. But they were terrified and affrighted, and supposed that they had seen a spirit. And he said unto them, Why are ye troubled? and why do thoughts arise in your hearts?"* (Luke 24:36-38).

If you are going to overcome fear, you have to go back and deal with those *thoughts* of worry and anxiety. Fear starts with questions such as, "What if they don't like me? What if something happens to my children, or my spouse? What if my business or my ministry does not succeed? What if I lose my job? "What if I don't ever get married?"

If you leave the marriage thought unchecked, before long, the devil will make sure you act on it. You'll pick up a newspaper and a front page article includes statistics that read, "The average woman over forty has a better chance of getting struck by lightening seven times on a Tuesday than getting married." This thought has now been birthed into your heart, and you fear that you are going to be alone the rest of your life.

The devil will then send some snaggletooth guy down your path with no job and still living in his mother's basement to profess that he loves you. "We can buy him some teeth!" you rationalize. That is fear talking. Don't let it drive you to make bad decisions.

Start praying what is found in Psalm 19:14 AMP: *"Let the words of my mouth, and the meditation of my heart, [your thoughts] be acceptable in thy sight, O Lord, my strength, and my redeemer."*

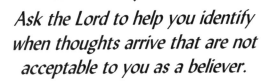

Ask the Lord to help you identify when thoughts arrive that are not acceptable to you as a believer.

He will shine the light of His Holy Spirit on the inside and show you when concepts or ideas are attempting to set themselves up in your heart that will eventually become destructive forces.

Next, let Scripture penetrate your very being. The psalmist writes, *"Thy word have I hid in mine heart, that I might not sin against thee"* (Psalm 119:11).

If you are going to cast down thoughts and replace them with the Word of God, it's essential that you know the Bible. Study the Scripture with purpose and research whatever area of challenge or temptation you are experiencing.

THE ACCOUNTABILITY FACTOR

Become accountable: to God, to yourself, and to others. We are told: *"Confess your faults one to another, and pray one for another, that ye may be healed. The effectual fervent prayer of a righteous man availeth much"* (James 5:16). The Amplified Bible says, *"Confess to one another therefore your faults (your slips, your false steps, your offenses, and your sins) and pray [also] for one another, that you may be healed and restored [to a spiritual tone of mind and heart]. The earnest (heart felt, continued) prayer of a righteous man makes tremendous power available [dynamic in its working]."*

There is no substitute for being answerable. But how do your become accountable to yourself? First, admit that there is nothing wrong with you just because you have this particular area of challenge at the moment. What is damaging is not dealing with the problem.

Don't let the devil heap condemnation on you. Ask God for a game plan to deal with the issue. You will find Him leading you to become accountable to God, yourself, and another human being.

There is tremendous power in having a fellow believer to whom you are responsible. I am not referring to a person with "loose lips"

40

who will spread your personal business, talk about you or look at you differently. I am also not suggesting a person who is going through the same trials you are encountering. You don't need someone who is slipping in the same area trying to help solve your problem. Find a godly individual who is strong and does not have a similar challenge. Be willing to let the Lord lead you to somebody that you can become vulnerable and accountable to. You want a person who is going to love you just as God does and not condemn you.

By putting these principles into practice, your anointed thoughts will not only be firmly planted, they will blossom and grow.

FOUR

ENVY AND JEALOUSY – DOUBLE TROUBLE

Some wonder why their lives are in a constant state of upheaval and disarray. It could be the result of an "evil work" which has entered their hearts through envy and jealousy.

Scripture is clear on the matter: *"For where envying and strife is, there is confusion and every evil work"* (James 3:16). When we leave this door open, the results can be disastrous.

For example, sickness is an evil work. You say, "Lord, hands have been laid on me ten times. I'm confessing Your Word. I am going to church and doing everything I believe I should as a Christian, and I still have not received my healing."

Could it be because there is envy and strife hidden in your heart?

This may also be the reason the door to poverty remains open. You pray, "Lord, I have been paying my tithes and claiming your promises. Why am I not experiencing prosperity in my finances?"

The same is true in relationships. "Why is there always confusion in my home?" You attend church; your husband or wife loves the Lord, yet you just can't seem to get along. Let me suggest you check the corners of your heart to make sure there is no envy or jealousy residing there.

43

THE "GREEN-EYED MONSTER"

Envy is the feeling of displeasure produced by witnessing or hearing of the advantage or prosperity of others.

Please understand, there is nothing wrong with desiring something you have seen someone else blessed with. We are supposed to be imitators of God; we should be striving everyday for our lives to look more and more like our heavenly Father. If I see my brother beginning to walk in a measure of God's blessing that draws him closer to the way the Lord expects our lives to look as believers, there is nothing wrong with wanting to walk in that same level of blessing.

The problem arises when I become upset because my brother is walking in favor I am not yet experiencing. Envy is not an issue when you are happy for someone who has received what you already possess.

———— ❖ ————

The "green-eyed monster" rears its ugly head when you become perturbed with a friend because of the blessings he or she may have received.

In the Amplified Bible we read, *"What leads to strife (discord and feuds) and how do conflicts (quarrels and fightings) originate among you? Do they not arise from your sensual desires that are ever warring in your bodily members? You are jealous and covet [what others have] and your desires go unfulfilled; [so] you become murderers. [To hate is to murder as far as your hearts are concerned.] You burn with envy and anger and are not able to obtain [the gratification, the contentment, and the happiness that you seek], so you fight and war. You do not have, because you do not ask"* (James 4:1-2).

The Word of God is telling us that we do not have to be upset—we can rejoice and be happy for one another. The reason you may not have what you desire is because your heart is not pure and clean enough to come before God and believe you can receive His blessing. The Lord may be telling you there are certain things you need to clean up or discard so you can approach the throne and say, "Father, I thank you that I also receive."

"WHAT ABOUT ME?"

The root of envy and jealousy is fear and selfishness—being only concerned with your life being blessed. It is extremely selfish when you become disturbed when someone else receives a blessing that they believed God for. Your only concern is, "Lord, what about me?"

When people are afraid of moving to a higher level, they often want to hold everyone else back. They would rather keep others as equal as possible—with the chance they could be seen as slightly superior. Many fear their friends will advance and leave them behind. It is the proverbial crab in a barrel: I am okay as long as we are all struggling.

In order to reach the place where you stop allowing jealousy to dominate your thinking, you are going to have to back up and start casting down not just feelings of envy, but also selfishness and fear.

Let me remind you again that the root of envy is the selfish feeling that *you* need to be blessed, not someone else—the fear that says the clock is ticking away and you still don't possess what you were expecting to have by now. You worry you will wind up

45

empty handed. If you understand this, you can begin to deal with the real cause and not allow it to control your thinking. As a result, you will be able to reach the level where you can actually be happy when others around you are being blessed.

THE HIDDEN DESTROYER

When you look at the exterior, you may not be able to see what is happening inside. Scripture gives this example during the time a new king was being sought for Israel: *"But the Lord said unto Samuel, Look not on his countenance, or on the height of his stature; because I have refused him: for the Lord seeth not as man seeth; for man looketh on the outward appearance, but the Lord looketh on the heart"* (1 Samuel 16:7).

Envy is not something you automatically see when you look at an individual. Many in church circles have learned how to put on the right face. We have practiced wearing the best smile and using the proper words when giving a testimony. We say, "Praise the Lord! God is good!" But often what we are really thinking is, "How did she get that?" and "When am I going to have mine?"

Jealousy is not always easy to detect. When you hear that Mary or Bob have been blessed, is there a quiet voice which says, "I deserve that more than they do" or "Every time something good takes place, it happens to them."

These are the whispers of covetousness that must be dealt with. Even though they may not seem major, remember, it is the small things that can begin to eat away and destroy you. It is like a person in the early stages of cancer. The man or woman can appear healthy, not knowing that a dreaded disease is eating away at their vital organs. The same thing is true with envy and jealousy. It is essential for you to detect the early warning signs and deal with them.

Scripture says, *"A calm and undisturbed mind and heart are the life and health of the body, but envy, jealousy, and wrath are like rottenness of the bones"* (Proverbs 14:30 AMP).

Some will not admit they are envious because they are not being honest with themselves. Think about the time when a church member said, "Look how God has blessed me." How did you truthfully feel at that moment? Did you respond, "Glory to God," but all along were cringing on the inside? Even if you felt this way only for a second, you cannot let it go unchecked.

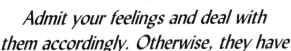

Admit your feelings and deal with them accordingly. Otherwise, they have the potential to ruin your life.

When God sees you rejoice with someone else, He will know you are ready to be blessed yourself.

PAYDAY IS COMING

Not only do we have to guard our hearts against becoming envious when other believers are being favored, but also when it happens to those who are not saved. When unbelievers acquire material possessions, it is not necessarily God who is blessing them. Sometimes it is because of the universal principle of sowing and reaping, or simply hard work—or because God is a merciful God. Personally, when I was unsaved and living like the devil, it was the goodness of God that led me to repentance.

When you work with people or have relatives who are not even pretending to live for God, yet it seems like they are successful and prospering, it may be difficult to understand. If you are not careful, you can become jealous of the unsaved. But remember what the Bible says, "*Let not thine heart envy sinners: but be thou in the fear of the Lord all the day long. For surely there is an end; and thine expectation shall not be cut off*" (Proverbs 23:17-18).

——— ❖ ———

Instead of being jealous of the sinner, keep walking in the fear of God, knowing that there will be a final accounting.

The Lord has a payday with your name on the account. Even if it doesn't seem you are walking in the full measure of His blessings at this moment, just keep living the right way. Continue to honor Him and He will see that your expectations are met.

WAIT FOR THE FATHER'S BEST

People who have gone through a divorce must be aware of the envy trap. I fully understand that when a marriage breaks apart there is usually blame on both sides. In many cases, ninety percent of the fault is with one person, but there is still at least some issues for which both partners are to blame.

Maybe your spouse committed adultery or was abusive and you are doing whatever it takes to raise the children. You then discover that your "ex" has remarried in less than a year. Now, because they have two incomes, they purchased a new house, but you are still living in an apartment struggling to pay the rent. One day you see them at the grocery store; they are stepping out of a shiny new car, dressed in expensive clothes. If you're not careful, envy will surface—especially if the spouse lied concerning their income so they wouldn't have to pay the full child support.

Remember, being envious will cause you to miss out on your blessing. Don't look at the offender and grumble, "They shouldn't have that. I'm the one who should be rewarded." Just declare that you know your day is coming. Wouldn't you rather have a future God's way? The Bible assures us, *"The blessing of the Lord, it maketh rich, and he addeth no sorrow with it"* (Proverbs 10:22). Even better, no man or system can take God's favor away from you.

The Lord knows how to deliver a mate, a house, a car, or a promotion to you. When it happens, lift your hands and praise the Lord. I would much rather wait and wait until I receive the Father's best than to bow my knee to the devil's plan.

TWO BROTHERS

There may be situations where you are envious of people in your own family. For example, parents can show favoritism toward one of their children, even though they shouldn't.

In Genesis 4 there is a story concerning two brothers, Cain and Abel. Cain didn't think it was necessary to do things God's way and believed he could make his own choices and succeed. In other words, his motives were not right.

Cain became jealous because the offering he presented to the Lord (based upon his own self-worth) was not acceptable, yet his brother's gift was. What Abel gave was received by God and he was rewarded accordingly. As the story continues we find that Cain became so green with envy that he killed his own brother.

This is a prime example of how jealousy can drive you to take matters into your own hands and commit an action you end up regretting.

49

"WHO DO YOU THINK YOU ARE?"

A similar scenario happened with Joseph and his siblings.

The young man was like many of us. He was so excited over what God was showing him as he slept that it caused him to speak prematurely. He exclaimed, "Oh my goodness, I dreamed a dream and all of you are bowing down to me" (Genesis 37).

If Joseph were your brother, you probably would have snidely remarked, "Huh, who do you think you are?"

His brothers were so consumed with jealousy they ended up selling him—their own flesh and blood—into slavery.

——— ❖ ———

*Don't be concerned over what God
is doing in someone else's life.*

If it seems the Lord is going to promote your brother or sister to a higher level than yourself, go ahead and say, "Well, praise God. Because of their blessing I am sure everyone will be blessed! If God is going to favor him, I know He has something great in store for me too!"

THE JEALOUS KING

In the account of David and Goliath, young David was able to slay the giant, not because he was bold and confident, rather, there was an anointing resting on his life.

Far too often, people become jealous or envious of someone without knowing why the person is blessed. Favor is the result of obeying the Lord and walking in His anointing. The Bible records, *"And David went out whithersoever Saul sent him, and behaved himself wisely: and Saul set him over the men of war, and he was accepted in the sight of all the people, and also in the sight of Saul's servants"* (1 Samuel 18:5).

Why was David accepted? There was a divine anointing on his life. We read. *"And it came to pass as they came, when David was returned from the slaughter of the Philistine, that the women came out of all cities of Israel, singing and dancing, to meet king Saul, with tabrets, with joy, and with instruments of musick. And the women answered one another as they played, and said, Saul hath slain his thousands, and David his ten thousands. And Saul was very wroth, and the saying displeased him; and he said, They have ascribed unto David ten thousands, and to me they have ascribed but thousands"* (verses 6-8).

SAUL "EYED" DAVID

When envy creeps into a person's heart, they begin to look at what God has done in their life as insignificant compared to another's. Their attitude shows resentment. Before "so-and-so" drove up in their brand new car, you were happy with your old clunker! In the case of David, the Bible tells us, *"And what can he have more but the kingdom? And Saul eyed David from that day and forward"* (verses 8-9.

Saul's jealously knew no bounds.

David was not running around flaunting his anointing, He was just doing what he was called to do—which included serving Saul.

Instead of King Saul being jealous over the touch of God on his servants' life, he should have been promoting the anointing he saw, allowing it to bless and minister to him.

I have observed pastors who make it a point to surround themselves with associates who are weak in the area of preaching.

They want to be able to go out of town and return to a congregation who says, "Oh pastor, please don't go on vacation again. While you were gone, this place just about fell apart."

I'm proud of the fact that everyone on my staff can probably out-teach and out-preach me. I am not worried if they do a great job while I am gone. In fact, I *anticipate* them doing well and expect people's lives to be blessed. The reason this does not intimidate me is because I understand and know who I am. People are still going to be saved and lives will be transformed. Their anointing becomes a benefit to me instead of a detriment and I thank God for their calling.

THE PLOT OF DESTRUCTION

Saul grew so jealous of David it escalated into rage. Scripture tells us, "*And it came to pass on the morrow, that the evil spirit from God came upon Saul, and he prophesied in the midst of the house: and David played with his hand, as at other times: and there was a javelin in Saul's hand. And Saul cast the javelin; for he said, I will smite David even to the wall with it. And David avoided out of his presence twice. And Saul was afraid of David, because the Lord was with him, and was departed from Saul*" (I Samuel 18:10-12).

What had David done to Saul that it resulted in attempted murder? Nothing!

———— ❖ ————

When envy and jealousy grow in a person's heart,
the problem can reach a point where you want to harm
whoever is walking around with what you covet.

A person may try what Saul did physically, but you can also wound and kill someone with vicious words. People give no thought to feelings and make comments such as, "Yes, they may have that expensive new home, but look at their marriage!" It may escalate to the level where they even stop associating with the object of their jealousy. Why? Because every time they are around them, they are reminded of what they wished they had. There is a war going on inside that is gnawing at their emotions.

CHECK YOUR HEART

Let me share from the Word what happened in the life of Saul:

So David fled, and escaped, and came to Samuel to Ramah, and told him all that Saul had done to him. And he and Samuel went and dwelt in Naioth. And it was told Saul, saying, Behold, David is at Naioth in Ramah. And Saul sent messengers to take David: and when they saw the company of the prophets prophesying, and Samuel standing as appointed over them, the Spirit of God was upon the messengers of Saul, and they also prophesied.

And when it was told Saul, he sent other messengers, and they prophesied likewise. And Saul sent messengers again the third time, and they prophesied also. Then went he also to Ramah, and came to a great well that is in Sechu: and he asked and said, Where are Samuel and David? And one said, Behold, they be at Naioth in Ramah. And he went thither to Naioth in Ramah: and the Spirit of God was upon him also, and he went on, and prophesied, until he came to Naioth in Ramah. And he stripped off his clothes also, and prophesied before Samuel in like manner, and lay down

naked all that day and all that night. Wherefore they say, Is
Saul also among the prophets? (1 Samuel 19:18-24).

God used Saul to give him a chance to recover from envy. That's
how the Lord is; He will give you an opportunity. Your heavenly
Father will place an individual or a situation in your path to help you
overcome and recover before your life is destroyed. This is why it is
so important to check your heart. God will give you chance after
chance to make things right, but there will come a point when you
will have to make the decision for yourself.

Saul was trying to catch David so that he could take his life. In
fact, he sent a group of messengers to find him. In the process,
God's anointing fell on them and they began to prophesy.

The Lord dispatched a second group of messengers to seek
David—and the anointing fell on them too. The same thing
happened with the third group: the anointing descended and they
also began to prophesy.

Eventually, Saul threw up his hands and said, "Forget it. I'm not
going to keep sending people."

Instead, he decided to find David himself. Then, when King Saul
was in the same area, he too began to speak prophetically. Here's
the point: the anointing had departed from Saul, but now it returned
to him. God demonstrated to Saul that if he would just get his heart
right, He would do the same thing for him that He had done in
David's life. God gave him a glimpse of how marvelous his journey
on earth could be.

The anointing which came on Saul was so strong that he
prophesied all day and night. It was so powerful that the people
were wondering if he was one of the prophets too. God was
attempting to show Saul that He was not doing a work in David
that He was not willing to do in his life.

---------- ❖ ----------

Don't become upset at the "Davids"
around you if you are not willing to take the
same positive, spiritual actions.

WHAT'S THE SECRET?

I've observed a minister becoming jealous of another pastor because of the way his church was growing. This has even been directed at me—a preacher upset because our congregation is flourishing. They complain we are stealing their members, as if I am standing out in front of their church on Sunday mornings with a gun!

If you visit a restaurant and they serve quality food, it is only natural you want to return. The same is true of churches. Some serve filet mignon while others only offer a ten minute SPAM® message every week.

If I were to find a ministry that had tremendous growth, I would want to sit down with that pastor and ask, "Would you mind telling me what you are doing that is causing your church to grow?"

I've had ministers come to say they've heard tremendous reports about our children's ministry and want to know if I could give advice and help them. We are grateful to God for our outreach in this area and have allowed our entire children's ministry team to go and train workers in other churches.

We are not trying to keep anything a secret. I want every church to grow because when they do it becomes much easier for us to be Christians in this world.

HANDLING JEALOUSY

Both David and Saul learned a powerful lesson: *"And it came to pass, when Saul was returned from following the Philistines, that it was told him, saying, Behold, David is in the wilderness of Engedi. Then Saul took three thousand chosen men out of all Israel, and went to seek David and his men upon the rocks of the wild goats. And he came to the sheepcotes by the way, where was a cave; and Saul went in to cover his feet: and David and his men remained in the sides of the cave"* (1 Samuel 24:1-3).

When Saul entered the cave to rest for the night he didn't know that David was in the back of this same cave.

This is an example of how you should handle a person who is jealous of you. In such a situation, the last thing you want to do is to lash out in retaliation.

Notice what took place in the lives of Saul and David:

And the men of David said unto him, Behold the day of which the Lord said unto thee, behold, I will deliver thine enemy into thine hand, that thou mayest do to him as it shall seem good unto thee. Then David arose, and cut off the skirt of Saul's robe privily. And it came to pass afterward, that David's heart smote him, because he had cut off Saul's skirt. And he said unto his men, The Lord forbid that I should do this thing unto my master, the Lord's anointed, to stretch forth mine hand against him, seeing he is the anointed of the Lord.

So David stayed his servants with these words, and suffered them not to rise against Saul. But Saul rose up out of the cave, and went on his way. David also arose afterward, and went out of the cave, and cried after Saul,

56

saying, My lord the king. And when Saul looked behind him, David stooped with his face to the earth, and bowed himself. And David said to Saul, Wherefore hearest thou men's words, saying, Behold, David seeketh thy hurt? Behold this day thine eyes have seen how that the Lord had delivered thee to day into mine hand in the cave: and some bade me kill thee: but mine eye spared thee; and I said, I will not put forth mine hand against my lord; for he is the Lord's anointed. Moreover, my father, see, yea, see the skirt of thy robe in my hand: for in that I cut off the skirt of thy robe, and killed thee not, know thou and see that there is neither evil nor transgression in mine hand, and I have not sinned against thee; yet thou huntest my soul to take it. The Lord judge between me and thee, and the Lord avenge me of thee: but mine hand shall not be upon thee.

As saith the proverb of the ancients, Wickedness proceedeth from the wicked: but mine hand shall not be upon thee. After whom is the king of Israel come out? after whom dost thou pursue? after a dead dog, after a flea. The Lord therefore be judge, and judge between me and thee, and see, and plead my cause, and deliver me out of thine hand (1 Samuel 24:4-15).

David was letting Saul know he could have killed him in that cave, but he had too much respect for the anointing on his life.

———— ❖ ————

You can easily become involved in a verbal war with someone who has been talking negatively about you on the job or even at church.

There may come a time when you are forced to confront and ask them why they are treating you this way. In the process, let them know that no matter how badly they act toward you, you are going to keep loving and blessing them because they are a member of God's family just as you are.

"JUST LET IT GO!"

When I first began going to the Word of Faith church in Detroit, there was a fellow who had been a member there for years. In fact, he grew up in that church.

I was just a young man who hardly anyone knew. Yet I was showing up for church every week and being faithful. I quickly was asked to be a part of the praise team and was grateful for the opportunity.

The word came to the attention of the pastor, Bishop Keith Butler, that I was walking upright before God. When I would minister he sensed the anointing on my life and, as a result, the pastor began to favor me.

At the same time, I began to notice this other man, who really didn't know me, would walk right past without speaking. My girlfriend (now my wife) and I would be sitting in the lobby and he would walk in the door and start talking with her without even acknowledging me.

There are levels of redemption, and in those early days I certainly wasn't at the level I am now. Where I come from, you don't just start talking to someone's girl—I don't care how long you have known each other.

This man would not even look at me or offer a "Hello. How are you doing?" My flesh would be rising and my girlfriend would later

LORD, SAVE ME FROM ME!

minister to me, saying, "Just let it go!"

Months went by and I did just that. I purposed in my heart I was going to love this man instead of allowing him to "bait" me in the flesh.

Here's what happened. He later became one of my biggest supporters and we are good friends to this day.

What if I had allowed myself to become lured into arguing back and forth with him? I would have placed myself in a position where we would have been fighting one another and probably not be friends today.

———— ❖ ————

God has called us to a higher lifestyle, so don't take the low road. Just keep loving and blessing others no matter what they do.

A TRAGIC ENDING

The Bible records how Saul's life abruptly came to a close. He asked for David's forgiveness, and I wish that were the end of the story. But a few chapters later, Saul had three thousand more men looking for David with the objective of killing him. In other words he had victory over his envy for a while, but jealously had such a hold on him, that when he let his guard down that old mentality washed back over him. As we discover:

Now the Philistines fought against Israel: and the men of Israel fled from before the Philistines, and fell down slain in Mount Gilboa. And the Philistines followed hard upon Saul and upon his sons; and the Philistines slew Jonathan, and

*Abinadab, and Malchi-shua, Saul's sons. And the battle went
sore against Saul, and the archers hit him; and he was sore
wounded of the archers.*

*Then said Saul unto his amourbearer, Draw thy sword, and
thrust me through therewith; lest these uncircumcised come
and thrust me through, and abuse me. But his armorbearer
would not; for he was sore afraid. Therefore Saul took a
sword, and fell upon it. And when his armorbearer saw that
Saul was dead, he fell likewise upon his sword, and died with
him. So Saul died, and his three sons, and his armor-bearer,
and all his men, that same day together* (1 Samuel 31:1-6).

Saul and his men were wiped out because he could not get over
the offense.

FOUR ESSENTIAL KEYS

Friend, we simply must rid ourselves of the scourge of envy and
jealously. We have to release these things and let them go
—regardless of where they may have been birthed. Perhaps it
started with your parents showing favoritism and now you feel you
are always the one being ignored. Take that fear out of your heart.
Have faith in God and believe He will deliver what He has promised.

Let me share four keys to overcoming envy and jealousy:

First: Thank God for how He has already blessed you.

The Bible says, *"In everything give thanks"* (1 Thessalonians
5:18).

At this very moment you have so much to give God thanks for.
Don't focus on what you *don't* have. Lift your hands and start
praising Him for what He has already blessed you with.

Second: Realize that everybody's life is different.

Scripture explains how we are all members of one Body even though we have different functions (1 Corinthians 12:14-27).

This indicates that each person has a unique anointing on his or her life. God's touch on one individual may cause certain blessings to come to them, but don't be influenced by this. Realize that you have a special anointing on your life as well.

You will receive everything the Almighty has destined for you as long as you keep walking in His will.

Third: Be a giver and learn to bless other people.

We are told to *"Rejoice with them that do rejoice"* (Romans 12:15). Don't become jealous when someone else receives God's favor. Join in on their blessing:

- If you learn someone has been blessed with a new house, ask if you can buy the very first welcome mat.
- If you discover a person has been blessed with a new car, volunteer to have it washed for them.
- If you find out a couple has just become engaged, ask if you can do anything to help make their wedding a success.

You are sowing seeds to keep the enemy from planting envy in your heart.

Fourth: Be aware that God is no respecter of persons.

We discover in the Word that God loves everyone equally (Romans 2:10-11). He does, however, honor obedience and faith.

61

If you are being faithful to what God has called you to and are walking in faith rather than fear, you will receive His outpouring of abundance.

Keep heaven's fire alive: *"That is why I would remind you to stir up (rekindle the embers of, far the flame of, and keep burning) the [gracious] gift of God, [the inner fire] that is in you by means of the laying on of my hands [with those of the elders at your ordination]."* (2 Timothy 1:6 AMP).

I pray you will start using these keys to overcome the double trouble of envy and jealousy.

FIVE

THE FEARS OF REJECTION AND FAILURE

I t's easy to recognize and deal with certain problems which are on the surface, but what we are dealing with requires digging down deep—getting to the heart of the matter. We have to pull back the covers and place ourselves under the fire of God's anointing.

This requires melting the wax, removing the fake "stuff," and getting down to the root, so we can be honest concerning what is going on in our hearts.

Many are bound by the fear of rejection and the fear of failing. But whenever we as believers have any type of anxiety operating in our lives, we have to deal with the issue, conquer it, and claim the victory! Fear is not something to take lightly; it is one of our worst enemies.

FACE WHAT FRIGHTENS YOU

Faith and fear are the exact opposites, and the Bible teaches that without faith, it is not possible to please God (Hebrews 11:6).

If a believer allows fear to govern their thinking, it will immobilize their ability to walk in faith and will leave them stuck in their present circumstances. You should never accept being afraid of anything—and that includes flying on an airplane. If you are scared to fly, try this. Buy an airline ticket as soon as possible and fly somewhere, even if it's a short thirty-minute flight. When you get to your destination turn around and fly back. If you are still afraid, repeat the process as soon as you can afford it!

I've met people who had a phobia of driving across bridges. If you live in our city, Jacksonville, Florida, such a person would be landlocked until they conquered that anxiety.

Public speaking is almost always rated as the number one fear. If you're frightened to stand and speak before a group, enroll in a speech class where you are taught the skills of giving presentations. I guarantee your anxiety level will decrease.

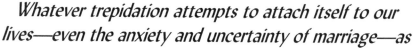

Whatever trepidation attempts to attach itself to our lives—even the anxiety and uncertainty of marriage—as believers, with God's help, we have to conquer it.

Start by being honest and identifying your fears, regardless of their size. If you fail to conquer "small" apprehensions, they will multiply and attempt to overtake you in other areas. Before you know what has happened, you won't just be afraid of the dark, but terrified of staying in your house alone!

THE FEAR OF REJECTION

We tend to repeat our behavior patterns so often that we don't recognize what is causing our response.

Since fear will not be satisfied until it controls every area of your life, be aware of the signals. Here are six indicators that will let us know we are walking in the fear of being rejected:

1. Consistently interpreting other people's actions as being negative toward you.

Have you ever met a person that, no matter what, they think the world is out to get them? I hope this doesn't describe you. Start seeing people as friends who want to support and encourage you—because in almost every case, they really do.

2. Living under the assumption you have offended those around you.

This is the individual who is always apologizing to everyone, usually for no good reason. One woman, who was standing in a room full of strangers, actually walked over to a guest and contritely said, "I've seen the way you have been looking at me, and want you to know that if I've done anything to offend you. I am so sorry."

It was the fear of rejection manifesting itself.

3. Creating a hard and tough exterior to keep from getting close to people.

Perhaps you work with men or women like this. They stay to themselves, not wanting to have any real interaction with anyone. Such individuals have concluded that the safest way to avoid rejection is to keep others at a distance. So they constantly build walls of protection, thinking, "How can someone turn me away if I don't make them a friend in the first place?"

4. Refraining from opening up and sharing with people how much you care about them.

There are those who have a difficult time saying the three most important words in the English language: "I love you." Men, especially, deal with this. For example, they want to tell their children how much they care for them, but when they try, it seems the words just won't naturally flow. In many cases, they have an unfounded fear of being rebuffed or turned away.

5. Trying to become friends with everybody, especially those who appear to be popular.

When a person has rejection anxiety, they will often identify with an individual who seems to be the most popular and try to immediately attach themselves. The assumption being, if they are friends with someone well-liked, they will be included too.

6. Having a very hard time saying "No."

Your mother calls and asks if you would help baby-sit her neighbors kids. You were planning to go out to dinner with your husband, but the minute you hesitate, she puts a guilt trip on you, saying, "You know, I went through labor with you for nineteen hours. You were the toughest of all my children to deliver."

Reluctantly, you give in, although *really* you wanted to say "No!"

When you are not afraid of being rejected by people, whoever they are, you can say, "Sorry, I can't do it this time."

THE FEAR OF FAILURE

On the other side of the coin is a condition that affects millions

—the fear of failure. How do you know if you have this problem?

1. You operate in a play-it-safe mode under the guise of wisdom.

It is wise to make sound, solid decisions in every area of your life. However, if you aren't careful, the fear of failure will cause you to never be willing to step out and take a chance—to lay it all on the line and risk everything. Instead, you will be inclined to disguise your hesitancy by saying, "Well, I am just using wisdom."

Thank God for wise judgment, but there are times when the Lord will speak to you boldly and strongly, asking you to step out and do something far beyond what your mind can conceive.

2. You want the best, but are always bracing for the worst.

Some people see the glass half full in *every* situation. When things are headed downhill, they think, "I knew this would happen." When things are going well, they wonder, "How long can this last?"

3. You constantly see yourself through the eyes of your past failures.

You may have had a baby out of wedlock as a teenager and everybody talked about you. Maybe your parents didn't handle the situation correctly. Now when you learn your young daughter is pregnant, there is no reason for you to disown her. There is nothing you can do to erase what has happened.

Instead of blaming your daughter and telling her to have an abortion, the best thing you can do is to throw your arms around her, love her, and prayerfully begin putting a plan together. Help her recover and move forward.

If you are a teenage mother, realize your mistake, turn your life around, and get back on track. The Lord offers forgiveness and wants you to be in fellowship with Him. Five, ten, or fifteen years down the road you will look back and see how this has brought you closer to God.

————— ❖ —————

Forget your past mistakes—the Lord certainly has. He says our sins are buried and will no longer be remembered against us (Hebrews 10:17).

4. You claim things beyond your control as your own personal failure.

There was no way you could have done anything to change the circumstance, but you end up taking the blame. In reality, it was not your fault in the first place.

WHY, LORD, WHY?

As a pastor, I have been confronted with many of these situations listed above, however, fear of rejection and fear of failure, are two I have had to deal with personally.

I grew up in what I thought was the perfect home—with a loving mother and father. Then, when I was eight years old, it seemed my whole world was shattered.

My parents decided they were going their separate ways, and I couldn't figure out why. Like most kids going through the trauma of the divorce of their parents, I wondered if it had anything to do with me.

For the next few years I had constant communication with my dad, nevertheless, I was still angry and confused because of my parent's separation. I desperately wanted my mother and father to get back together, remarry, and all of us live happily ever after.

Whenever my mom would come close to having a relationship with someone new, I would show signs of rebellion, hating the very thought of another man coming into my life.

I remember the time my mother would bring a friend to the house that she had been seeing. Before his arrival, she'd say, "I want you to meet him so you can tell me what you think."

Before the doorbell rang, I would be in the bedroom, trying to come up with the meanest possible look on my face. When I was introduced, I wouldn't even speak to him—and would have preferred a whipping!

My little brother, five years younger, would come out bouncing all over the place with a big smile on his face. I was so mad at him because he was supposed to be on my side!

During these years, I was developing anger and confusion in my heart.

THE SECOND HAMMER

Years later, my mom met her second husband and they were married. Fortunately, I really loved him and believed life was returning to what I remembered as a child. As time went by, my mother had two more children—and I had another brother and a sister. I became comfortable with this man in my life, and he instilled wonderful principles in me. I warmed up enough to be willing to call him "Dad." That was a big step!

Then dropped the second hammer! My new dad was in the

military and, for whatever reason, he and my mother split up and went their separate ways.

I was more than upset. Instantly, as a teenager, I knew it was going to be more difficult to open up and trust again. I was not willing to allow anyone else other than my mother and immediate family ever to get close enough for me to experience a broken heart once more.

Although, the pain I felt wasn't visible, I was hurting deeply. However, I covered it well and maintained positions of leadership throughout school—captain of my basketball and baseball team, receiving accolades on the football field and headed up a singing group.

To the casual observer, I appeared to be doing well, but I had built a wall around my heart, determined to never let myself be rejected or pushed away again.

Spiritually, I drew closer to the Lord, knowing He would never let me down

After being married and graduating from Bible school I was hired full time as a minister at the Word of Faith church in Detroit, Michigan. Shortly thereafter, Bishop Keith Butler observed my diligence in serving the Lord and he began mentoring and tutoring me. Without question, this was God's favor as Bishop Butler began to impart spiritual wisdom into my life.

The personal time I spent with him developed me far beyond what I had ever known. He deposited within me things of the Spirit I didn't receive from my father or my stepfather.

Even after all of this, there was still a wall of restraint between me and any other person—including Bishop Butler.

WOULD IT HAPPEN AGAIN?

The Word of God, if sown into your heart, will uncover everything. I am sharing this with you now because I can look back and see what was truly happening. At the time I didn't know.

During those years in Detroit, for some reason, I would only allow myself to just get so close to Bishop Butler, and no closer.

He was opening up doors for me and being a blessing to my life. Then one evening I confided to my wife, "I am blessed with what is happening at church, but I have a fear in my heart that one day I am going to do or say something and Bishop Butler is going to stop our relationship. If that happens, I'll end up having another male figure in my life who I highly respect cut me off again."

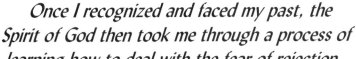

*Once I recognized and faced my past, the
Spirit of God then took me through a process of
learning how to deal with the fear of rejection.*

I am happy to report it has been many years since that time, and I have never had to deal with the problem again. It's so much better being free than having every relationship in my life affected because of the fear that someone is not going to accept me.

Once I came to the place where I conquered this fear, I was empowered to have relationships that were not like nooses around my neck. I became liberated to love people and enjoy them.

PLAYING IT SAFE?

Please allow me to make a personal confession.

When I began writing this book, the Spirit of God began to deal with me, telling me that I had been operating under a fear of failure. I thought to myself, "Fear of failure? What do you mean? I have never failed at anything."

I am not saying that to be boastful, but I haven't. I have been blessed—having achieved in academics, sports, and have enjoyed wonderful relationships.

Nevertheless, the Spirit of God began showing me that I had been functioning in the play-it-safe mode. The Lord revealed that I had certain "safe guards" in place to make sure that if He did not come through, I had a back up plan. He told me I had operated in great faith and had achieved much, but that I had placed myself in a position that even if His power did not fully move, I had enough safety nets under me that I wouldn't hit rock bottom.

As He began opening my eyes to these things, I had to step back and be honest with myself. That's when I realized I had been living under a fear of failure.

When you have enjoyed accomplishments and successes over extensive periods, sometimes there is a fear of "What if I step out, follow God, and do exactly what He tells me to do and things don't work out"?

Those negative thoughts can grip your heart and cause you to operate under a cloud of fear even though it may not be visible on the outside.

DEAL WITH IT!

I share my testimony not because God obligates me to, but I want you to realize that ministers are human too. There is a place for honoring ministry gifts, but sometimes we can end up placing those in the Lord's work on a pedestal. People who serve in the capacity of a pastor, prophet, or evangelist have to deal with the same kind of human challenges everyone else has to face. We are no different.

———————— ❖ ————————

Once we identify a personal fear, whatever it is, we have to be unrelenting in its annihilation.

It is essential that we open our hearts and ask God, "Please Father, speak to me. I recognize the problem and with Your help I will deal with it."

"RIGHT STANDING"

In order to overcome both the fears of failure and rejection, you have to build your life on a foundation of righteousness—which means "right standing." The Word tells us:

> *You shall establish yourself in righteousness (rightness, in conformity with God's will and order): you shall be far from even the thought of oppression or destruction, for you shall not fear, and from terror, for it shall not come near you. Behold, they may gather together and stir up strife, but it is not from Me. Whoever stirs up strife against you shall fall and surrender to you.*
>
> *Behold, I have created the smith who blows on the fire of coals and who produces a weapon for its purpose; and I have created the devastator to destroy. But no weapon that is formed against you shall prosper, and every tongue that shall rise against you in judgment you shall show to be in the*

wrong. This [peace, righteousness, security, triumph over opposition] is the heritage of the servants of the Lord [those in whom the ideal Servant of the Lord is reproduced]; this is the righteousness or the vindication which they obtain from Me [this is that which I impart to them as their justification], says the Lord (Isaiah 54:14-17 AMP).

When you establish yourself in righteousness, it causes you to begin seeing who you are in Christ instead of the person you are in the flesh. As Paul wrote to the believers at Corinth, *"Consequently, from now on we estimate and regard no one from a [purely] human point of view [in terms of natural standards of value]. [No] even though we once did estimate Christ from a human viewpoint and as a man, yet now [we have such knowledge of Him that] we know Him no longer [in terms of the flesh]"* (2 Corinthians 5:16 AMP).

In other words, after salvation, we do not identify with people simply based on their carnal nature or outward appearance. Think about it. We no longer need to pay attention to anyone based on their hair style, skin color, how much education they do or do not have, or how much money is in their bank account.

We must start seeing the way God does—and He looks at the heart. If the Almighty tells me not to know anyone based on the flesh—that includes me! I must no longer view myself in terms of my skills, my career, or my possessions. There is only one measuring stick: am I in right standing with God?

This is a powerful question.

Many of us have heard phrases from the pulpit for so long it becomes "religiosity" and we don't stop to consider what it truly means. I trust you know what it is to have God say you are in right standing with Him.

AN IMPORTANT ENCOUNTER

If the President of the United States personally phoned you, can you imagine what an honor it would be to speak with him? If he invited you to the Oval Office and began telling you how he had heard good things concerning you and the great works you have contributed to your community, your chest would be bursting with pride. It would feel indescribable to know you are in right standing with the President—and when you leave his office to return home, you would probably be walking on air! Your life would be changed.

The experience would impact you in such a positive way that if a friend said even one discouraging word, you would brush it off, telling yourself, "I'll just pray for them." After all, you had talked with the President. In your heart, you would feel justified, as if you had made it—you had arrived!

Although your Oval Office visit would be an honorable accomplishment, there is someone far greater than any president, prime minister, or king who has declared you are in right standing with Him.

——— ❖ ———

Because you have confessed Jesus Christ as your Lord and are a member of His family, God Almighty has proclaimed that you are now righteous before Him.

This changes everything. The Lord promises, "Not only will I bless you, I will promote you and raise you higher. I will always be by your side."

75

No Longer Afraid

Since God says you are in right standing with Him, why allow any man or woman to determine how you feel about yourself?

You must never permit situations to dictate how you will respond to circumstances. If you call someone and they do not return your phone call, don't feel slighted. If you're single, go on a date and the person never calls you again, don't feel insignificant. Why let trivial incidents affect how you feel about yourself and others when you have God Almighty!

Of course, I want to make sure I don't offend people or behave in a way that causes them to shun me, but I do not lose any sleep at night if another individual does not like me. When all is said and done, I am going to have to stand before God. As long as I can go to bed at night knowing I have gone well beyond the call of duty of being pleasing unto Him, everyone else has to take a number.

Certainly, I want people to attend our church; I think it is one of the greatest congregations you'll ever find. Not because of me, but because the undiluted Word of God is being taught. However, I recognize our church is not for everyone. Some may feel more comfortable worshiping elsewhere.

More than Crowds

When we started Faith Christian Center in Jacksonville, Florida, we only had about three to five rows of people in a small church building. If two or three families decided to visit their loved ones on the same day as a church service, there would hardly be anyone left in the congregation. At first we roped off the back pews so those who attended would sit in the front.

We could tell how the church was growing because week after week we kept moving the ropes back one more row. Glory to God!

I remember one particular Sunday when I felt I had preached my finest sermon. My flesh said, "People are going to be in here in droves next week."

I figured after a message like that, our members were going to bring everyone they knew to church. When next Sunday rolled around, half of the folks didn't show up, they must have been out of town. Our attendance was lower than it had ever been during that time.

When I stood up to minister, my mind was in turmoil. I was in the pulpit trying to praise God and at the same time attempting to figure out where all those people went!

After the service, on my way home, I cried, "Lord, I need you to tell me what I did wrong." God was silent. When He finally spoke, about two or three days later, the only thing He said was, "Preach the Word. Be instant in season and out of season."

From that day forward, I paid no attention to how many people were in the congregation. I have learned when we have a full house, God is there! And when people for one reason or another are not present, He is there too! I am going to preach the same way. Even if there were just one row of people, I would stand and preach my heart out. Thank God, His Word never changes.

WHOSE APPROVAL COUNTS?

If you see yourself only through the eyes of your successes or failures, you will either become prideful or end up with low self-esteem, thinking you don't measure up. You must view your life through the eyes of Christ. As long as you are doing your best and

77

giving it all to God, whatever the results, He will be satisfied. You do not have to exist bouncing up and down based on a barometer of what someone else thinks.

Learn to love and trust people and always be willing and prepared to serve others. We all need one another, but when it comes to seeking approval or a pat on the back, we must grow to a place where we do not require being applauded by man.

It's a great feeling when we are acknowledged, but we cannot live our lives based on praise or criticism.

WHAT DOES GOD THINK?

Many years ago, the Lord impressed upon me two verses of Scripture that set me free from the opinion of others: *"But when He was in Jerusalem during the Passover Feast, many believed in His name [identified themselves with His party] after seeing His signs (wonders, miracles) which He was doing"* (John 2:23 AMP).

When the people saw the miracles and ministry of Jesus, they gravitated to Him. Likewise, when others see you doing an excellent job, they are attracted to you. People enjoy being around success, but you want loyal friends who will stick by you through good times and bad. Some may applaud, but are they really on your team?

In the next verse we read: *"But Jesus [for His part] did not trust Himself to them, because He knew all [men]"* (verse 24 AMP),

The Lord ministered to them, loved them, blessed their lives, and served them well, but He did not place His trust in man. In other words, Jesus did not allow His sense of self-worth, self-esteem, or

78

His ability to be entrusted to the opinion of men and women. Jesus made certain His performance was based solely on what His heavenly Father thought.

Far too often we become servants to the opinion of others, even if we do so unconsciously. For example, we may sing a solo in church, then hang around at the end of the service just to hear what people thought.

The reason I know this is true is because I used to do the exact same thing! I grew up singing in Detroit and our group participated in midnight musicals at Bailey's Cathedral. There were great gospel artists who would minister, including Mattie Moss Clark, Commissioned, the Winans, the Clark Sisters, and our group, "All For Christ."

When our turn came, we would sing our teenage hearts out, doing our best to glorify God! However, when the evening was over, we would wait around to hear what people were saying. If someone commented, "You really blessed me," we would respond, "Oh praise God," knowing all along we were really waiting for a compliment.

We didn't recognize it at the time, but we were committing ourselves to people, allowing our sense of self-worth to rise, fall, or stay the same based on what others thought. We should have arrived prayed up, thoroughly rehearsed, and only concerned with ministering unto the Lord—then leaving the rest to the Holy Spirit.

YOU'VE BEEN ADOPTED

Instead of hearing good reports, many believers have been beaten down over the years by the words of their relatives or teachers who did not know the right way to minister to them. All their lives they were constantly being told, "You will never amount

79

to anything," or "You are going to be just like your daddy—you even look like him."

More than one pregnant teenager has been told, "You're going to keep on having babies—that's all you are good for."

I've met young people in our church who were adopted, and for their whole life they have struggled, trying to figure out why they were pushed out of their biological parents' home.

If this paints a picture of your past, settle it in your mind once and for all that perhaps it had nothing to do with them. Maybe God loved you enough to know that if He did not intervene and pull you out of that situation; you would not have found Him when you did.

There are some things we ascribe to the devil that Satan could never take credit for if he tried. God implements enough providence in our lives to intervene and remove us from disastrous circumstances. So, don't feel rejected when the Lord chooses to change your environment. Why? Because He has something far greater in store for your future.

As a believer, you have been adopted into the family of God and are a son or daughter of the Most High. As a result, you are an heir to everything your Father possesses.

The Lord will replace your fear of rejection with His love and compassion. He will turn your fear of failure into a faith that will last for eternity. Now this is worth getting excited about!

SIX

OUT OF THE COMFORT ZONE

It is essential to develop a can-do mentality. We cannot afford to walk around afraid of failing. As I tell people, "If you are going to fail, fail going forward."

This is the attitude I have adopted. I would rather make mistakes attempting to obey God than just sitting in the boat talking about who is going to walk on the water. Remember Peter? He risked everything by putting his feet in the sea. In fact, he went down into the water, but came back up walking with Jesus.

Among the disciples, Peter is the only one we have a record of who walked on water. Why? Because he was willing to fail.

Are you prepared to obey the Lord and take such a risk?

The apostle Paul wrote, *"I have strength for all things in Christ Who empowers me [I am ready for anything and equal to anything through Him Who infuses inner strength into me; I am self-sufficient in Christ's sufficiency]"* (Philippians 4:13 AMP).

"YOU ARE DOING WHAT?"

When I left Michigan State University, I was a mechanical

81

engineering student with a 3.3 grade point average. I was offered a position at General Motors, who promised that when I graduated they would bring me on board full-time and promote me through the ranks as an engineer.

I was told I had the qualities they were looking for and the whole plan was laid out before me. But God in His infinite wisdom came along and began to change everything. He told me He didn't want me to finish school at that particular time, or work for General Motors. Instead, the Lord said, "I want you to enroll in Bible school to train for the ministry."

That was God's plan. "However, my objective was to finish college, go to work for General Motors, and after saving a substantial amount of money, I would then take a year or two leave of absence, and go to Bible school. That way, if things didn't work out, I could always return to my job at GM.

My carefully thought-out blueprint had to take a back seat. I knew the Lord was serious when He said it was time to leave—and I decided to obey His call.

Most of my friends thought I was crazy. "You are doing what? You are leaving a future with General Motors to study for the ministry? To be a preacher?"

"Yes," I replied. "I am going to Bible school because that is what God is telling me."

A SPECIAL ASSIGNMENT

I left Michigan State, said goodbye to the opportunity at General Motors, and enrolled in Bible school. I had nothing to hang onto—no plan B or C.

If things didn't work out, I was going to look like the biggest fool of the century, but I was willing to risk everything and obey

God. I decided I was not going to play it safe, miss my window of opportunity and let God give my future in ministry to someone else.

Had I not stepped out when I did, I would not have been ready when it was time to open the church I now pastor in Jacksonville, Florida. The Lord could have called someone else for the task who may have been a success, but it would not have been me. I would have missed my opportunity and my assignment.

—————— ❖ ——————

It is vital not to be paralyzed and gripped with fear wondering whether or not you are doing the right thing.

WHAT IS NEXT?

There are some who refuse to get involved with relationships because they have had a bad previous experience. You may have had a loveless marriage and gone through a difficult divorce. Perhaps your spouse was abusive and didn't treat you with respect. Now fear has seized your heart and you do not know if you want to enter into a relationship again because you might choose the wrong person—as you did in the past.

However, God is able to bring a wonderful individual into your life and give you a new beginning. Don't close you heart to what the Lord may be preparing. Remember, God has not given you the spirit of fear. He has ordained total victory for you!

Normally when people talk about habits in the flesh, they refer to smoking drinking, and cursing. Although these have to be dealt with, we are addressing the things that are not so easily seen.

If we could peel back the curtain of this natural realm and have a glimpse through the Spirit to see what God has lined up for our lives in the next five years, we would get busy making sure there was nothing going on inside of us that would disqualify us from walking in those blessings.

God has been allowing me to see just a small portion of what He wants to do in my life and in my family. I have purposed in my heart not to allow anything to interfere with what He is planning.

Let me ask you to repeat this prayer with me:

In the name of Jesus, I am asking, Lord, save me from me. I am declaring that it is not my mother, father, husband, or wife. It is not my children or my job, and it is definitely not the devil because he is already defeated. Lord, I need you to save me from me. I am asking you to help me get over being selfish, greedy, lazy, and prideful and from isolating myself from You. Help me to become all that You have ordained for my life. I know You have an awesome plan for me and my loved ones. In the name of Jesus, I will walk in it.

From this moment forward, listen carefully. If God asks you to leave your comfort zone, don't hesitate. His divine purpose and plan is always the best.

SEVEN

MURMURING AND COMPLAINING

I remember a recent time in Florida when we were in a drought and hardly had any rain. Fires were igniting in fields across the state and the officials were forced to shut down one of the Interstate highways for several days because there was too much smoke. People were complaining, "I've never seen it this dry!"

Not long after, there was a period when the skies opened up and we were being drenched every day. Now the residents were asking, "When is this rain going to stop?"

In August, people complain about the heat and humidity; in January, it's too cold. Is this how God wants His children to act—always fault-finding?

According to the Word, the Lord expects us to be different from the world. As Paul writes, *"[Not in your strength] for it is God Who is all the while effectually at work in you [energizing and creating in you the power and desire], both to will and to work for His good pleasure and satisfaction and delight. Do all things without grumbling and faultfinding and complaining [against God] and questioning and doubting [among yourselves]"* (Philippians 2:13-14 AMP).

Two words of this passage stand out: "all things." The Lord is telling us we should live without a grumbling attitude.

Unfortunately, murmuring and complaining are two habits which run so deep into the psyche and personality that many people do not even recognize how much time they spend doing it. The word murmuring in New Testament Greek means complaining or faultfinding. The dictionary defines it as "uttering complaints in a low voice or a gloomy and sour manner."

THE FAULT FINDERS

The world is notorious for negative expressions, but as believers we should be light in the midst of darkness. God expects us to be the exact opposite of what we see in our culture and society.

At work, you probably spend eight or more hours every day with people who complain about everything:

- "I haven't had a raise in two years?"
- "Why don't they buy some new equipment for us to work with?"
- "Why are we required to work mandatory overtime?"
- "How come the boss doesn't speak to me?

Sadly, it's not always just the other person who is griping. If I were to follow you home, listen to your conversations and how you handle your business, I can almost guarantee I could find some fault. That's human nature. However, God has given us a choice. We can either constantly be dissatisfied and murmuring, or we can live our lives as the Bible teaches: *"In every thing give thanks"* (I Thessalonians 5:18).

IT'S A COMMAND!

You've probably met Christians who you consider to be champions. They love the Lord, read His Word, and serve Him, yet they seem to have one major flaw—expressing their displeasure with things going on around them.

———— ❖ ————

When God says, "Don't murmur or complain," this is a command!

Let's put it in practical terms. Husbands are to take care of their responsibilities without grumbling or fault finding. They should not arrive home from work bemoaning the fact that they are the primary bread-winner of the family. Some also bring home their displeasure: "Don't you think I should be greeted in a clean house sometimes?" Yes, you should, but according to the Word, you don't have a right to murmur or complain about it.

Wives have a different view. They respond, "Well, I've been slaving all day, too—taking care of the kids, cooking, and washing clothes."

Instead of complaining, commit to prayer and ask the Lord to help you overcome the sin of finding fault. Our lifestyle should conform to the Word in every aspect—at home or at work.

Employers should not despair or worry over what their workers are *not* doing. Instead, they should set the objectives and encourage people to reach them. If not, rather than complaining about their inadequacies, perhaps they should be let go.

As an employee, if you are unhappy at work, either stay on the job and stop murmuring or quit and go somewhere else—but you don't have a right to remain and constantly complain.

DON'T CLOG THE PIPELINE

Perhaps you've been stuck for an hour in heavy traffic on the freeway. Or you ran into the grocery store to pick up an item or two, and the line snaked all the way to the back aisle. In that situation you have to make a conscious decision. You can either stand in line with a smile, or put the groceries down and leave.

At such times it's difficult to remember that, according to the Word, murmuring and complaining is a sin.

———— ❖ ————

Without repenting, it will clog the pipeline of blessing and keep us from receiving and becoming all God has ordained for us.

TAKE IT TO THE TOP!

Recently, my wife and I were flying home from Detroit and I was meditating on this subject. I opened my Bible and showed her the scripture in Philippians where it tells us to do all things without murmuring. "What do you think about that?" I asked her.

"Those words are really tough," she responded. And, in the natural, it truly is.

If there is something we don't like, we are quick to express our displeasure, I am not saying when things are going wrong you should *always* zip you lip and never utter one word. But there is a right way and proper time to deal with anything. Take it to the top! If you are going to talk about what is happening on the job or in the ministry, you need to approach a person in leadership who can address the issue rather than gossiping on the topic with others. Most important, you should be talking to God!

When you bring the matter to the Lord, He will begin by

focusing on you—and how you need to respond differently.

One day in prayer, God clearly spoke to my spirit, saying, "If your words are not part of the solution, then your words are adding to the problem."

"RIGHTEOUS" TALK

It is far better to close our lips than to talk about a situation in a negative way. Most of us know that Solomon, the richest and wisest king on record, is credited for writing the book of Proverbs. He wrote these profound words: *"Hear; for I will speak excellent and princely things; and the opening of my lips shall be for right things. For my mouth shall utter truth, and wrongdoing is detestable and loathsome to my lips. All the words of my mouth are righteous (upright and in right standing with God); there is nothing contrary to truth or crooked in them"* (Proverbs 8:6-8 AMP).

Solomon was committed to "righteous" talk. If this wise and wealthy man came to this conclusion, could it be possible there is a direct connection between wisdom and prosperity and being able to keep our mouth from speaking evil?

The apostle Paul tells us, *"Let no corrupt communication proceed out of your mouth, but that which is good to the use of edifying, that it may minister grace unto the hearers"* (Ephesians 4:29). The Amplified version translates, *"Let no foul or polluting language, nor evil nor unwholesome or worthless talk [ever] come out of your mouth; but only such [speech] as is good and beneficial to the spiritual progress of others, as it is fitting to the need and the occasion, that it may be a blessing and give grace (God's favor) to those who hear it."*

It's easy to engage in trivial conversation. You might not be cursing, lying, or verbally tearing apart anyone's reputation or character, but sometimes we sit around and talk about things which have little or no value. The Bible tells us to guard our tongue and not let any foul, unwholesome, or worthless conversation come out of our mouth.

WORD POWER

For many, if they eliminated all of their unclean and worthless chatter, they wouldn't have much to say. But we are called to be different. Our tongues were created to praise God and testify to His goodness.

The Bible includes this nugget of truth:, *"With his mouth the godless man destroys his neighbor, but through knowledge and superior discernment shall the righteous be delivered"* (Proverbs 11:9 AMP).

Have you ever known a person whose self-esteem has been destroyed because of someone else's careless words? Perhaps you have suffered this way because you were constantly told what you could not do or berated for your actions.

Your parents may have loved you with all of their hearts, but did not know how to minister life to your spirit, so they constantly complained how horrible your grades were and criticized the foolish mistakes you were making. The more they did this, the worse things became.

The Bibles says that a hypocrite destroys his neighbor with his words but the just are delivered once they obtain knowledge. When you learn that every word you utter has power, it puts an entirely different spin on what you will and will not say. Scripture tells us, *"Reckless words pierce like a sword, but the tongue of the wise brings healing"* (Proverbs 12:18 NIV). And we know that *"He that keepeth his mouth keepeth his life: but he that openeth wide his lips*

LORD, SAVE ME FROM ME!

shall have destruction" (Proverbs 13: 3).

Many people would be alive today if they had just kept their thoughts to themselves. As the Word declares, *"A fool's lips enter into contention, and his mouth calleth for strokes. A fool's mouth is his destruction, and his lips are the snare of his soul. The words of a talebearer are as wounds, and they go down into the innermost parts of the belly"* (Proverbs 18:6-8), The Amplified version says, *"His mouth invites a beating."*

Perhaps you have met people who talk so much, it's as if their mouths are screaming, "Slap me, please slap me!" Remember, *"Death and life are in the power of the tongue: they that love it shall eat the fruit thereof"* (Proverbs 18:21).

Verse after verse in the book of Proverbs, Solomon teaches on the power of the words we speak. In my Bible, I have those verses highlighted. If this wise and prosperous man is telling me I need to control my tongue, then I need to stop and pay attention.

AN ENCOURAGING WORD

There are marriages that would not be on such shaky ground if both parties would learn how to stifle their words—including talking about divorce.

––––––––– ❖ –––––––––

When things are tough, never let your emotions back you into a corner and cause you to say something you do not really mean.

For the born again believer, divorce is not an option, especially if there is no adultery involved. You do not have a right to end your marriage just because things "aren't working out."

91

Let your words be those that build and encourage instead of tear down and destroy. When you speak to someone do so with love and positive expressions. No one likes to be constantly criticized for what they are doing wrong.

Wives, if you want your husband to help more around the house, stop complaining how long it takes him to finish a job. Speaking personally, if you let a man think the idea is his, he will run through a troop and leap over a wall to do what you ask.

Let me share a secret. If your husband only does part of a job and you want him to complete the task, try this. When he comes through the door and you are on the phone with your sister, girlfriend, or mother, start bragging about the job he has started. You might say, "I asked Roger to plant some flowers for me and, oooh, you haven't seen anything like these. Our neighbor's flowers are drooping all over the place, but the ones Roger planted are amazing. All I did was ask him and he went out and dug up the weeds and really did a super job."

Roger, standing in the doorway, will say to himself, "Yeah, I did do that, didn't I?" And before you know it, he will come into the house, change his clothes and rush back outside and start digging again.

The same is true of women. Every now and then she wants to hear how much you like her cooking. She may not cook often, but when she does, brag to your friends and tell them how delicious it was. Your words of praise will get back to her in a hurry.

Your family is precious, and you don't want to refer to them in a negative light. In truth, they are part of you, and when you speak of them disparagingly, you are actually talking about yourself.

A PAT ON THE BACK

Another concern I have is that believers should not be verbally tearing down their church. It's human nature that when things are going well, we have little to say. However, when they don't go the way we think they should, our tongues begin to wag.

This is not God's way.

—————— ❖ ——————

Your place of fellowship is where the Lord has sent you to learn the Word and to worship, not to complain and gossip.

The reason I am committed to giving members of our congregation "a pat on the back" is because it helps reaffirm their significance and assists in their spiritual growth. When I attend minister's conferences, I'm constantly bragging on my church family. They are men and women committed to the Lord and faithful to ministry.

Some pastors speak of how their congregations fall asleep during service. I quickly let them know, "We don't have that problem. Our members come to church awake, expecting to receive a Word from the Lord." When a person's expectancy is high they will listen intently, encouraging the preacher to deliver even more.

I am often asked, "What are you doing to get keep your people coming back?" My answer is, I am teaching the Word, encouraging our staff, loving our members, and praising the Lord!

I have learned that men and women may not be perfect, but a little admiration goes a long way. That's why I make an extra effort to applaud our Ministry of Helps workers.

A SERIOUS MATTER
The Bible warns us, *"Touch not mine anointed"* (Psalm 105:15).

So I refuse to allow anyone to disrespect a church member in my presence. Sure, we esteem those who stand behind the sacred desk, but the Lord's anointed includes every born again believer in the Body of Christ.

———— ❖ ————

If I find myself criticizing my brother, I have actually spoken negatively about Jesus.

Remember, Christ said, *"Inasmuch as ye have done it unto one of the least of these my brethren, ye have done it unto me"* (Matthew 25:40).

To give you a better idea how serious this matter is in the sight of God—and what consequences may result, read these words of the apostle Paul: *"That [careless and unworthy participation] is the reason many of you are weak and sickly, and quite enough of you have fallen into the sleep of death"* (1 Corinthians 11:30 AMP).

When you study this verse in its context, Paul is saying there are many who are sick and have died prematurely because they did not rightly discern the body of Christ—every born again believer.

This should cause you to stop in your tracks and ask yourself if you should be commenting on a matter when you don't know all the facts. How much better to keep quiet and pray for the situation. Of course, the minute the Lord begins to minister to you regarding this, the devil will devise a scheme to test you.

"WHERE'S MY LUGGAGE?"

While preparing to teach this message to our congregation, my wife and I were flying into Jacksonville from a trip. The more I thought about the subject, my spirit began to leap. I told my wife,

LORD, SAVE ME FROM ME!

"If I had a parachute, I could jump out right here and start preaching!"

We were excited to be home because we had been gone for two weeks. As soon as we landed, I went to retrieve our luggage and my wife headed for an exit area on the other side of the airport to wait for me.

One bag came out and I grabbed it, then came the second. Since my wife was on this trip, we had to travel with at least three bags!

As I waited, the carousel circled around and around—and then it stopped. I ran over to the airline representative and asked, "Is that it!?"

"Yes," He replied. "If something's missing you'll need to check at the baggage claim office."

I was disappointed, having done all this traveling, making it home safely, and now I was missing one piece of luggage."

Then I thought about the message I was going to preach the next morning—about murmuring and complaining. So I headed over to the office with a big smile on my face. There were two people ahead of me and the attendant was on the phone.

When he finally hung up and took care of the other travelers, I told him my plight. "Let me see your claim check," he asked politely.

Then I realized those stubs were on the other side of the airport with my wife. Oh me! But I bit my tongue and didn't complain.

By the time I reached my wife and returned with the claim check, the clerk was on the telephone again and three more people were in front of me!

Finally, after giving the attendant everything he asked for, he said, "I'm sure your bag will be on the next flight in. We'll deliver it to your house."

With the same smile on my face we headed home and I

continued preparing my message on the folly of murmuring and complaining.

WAITING FOR BUBBA!

That Saturday night, about 10:00 P.M., I received a call from the airline and the agent told me the plane had landed and they had my bag. Then he said, "We will call you in a few minutes to let you know the delivery time."

I thought, "It looks like I still have time to get the bag and be in bed at a decent hour."

To my dismay, sixty minutes went by and no one had called. Finally, a guy named Bubba phoned and said he would be delivering the luggage, but needed some directions. He told me he was heading out and would be at my house in a little while.

The airport is less than half an hour from where we live. So, while waiting, we dozed off—leaving the television on so we wouldn't fall into too deep a sleep. At 3:00 A.M. I looked at my watch. There was no Bubba and no bag anywhere to be found. Finally, a few minutes later, our doorbell rang. All the way to the front door I kept practicing what I was preparing to preach, "I will not murmur or complain."

I smiled at Bubba and said, "Thanks!"

The next morning I woke up a little tired physically, but refreshed in my spirit because I refused to allow myself to become agitated and lured into finding fault. I walked into the pulpit with a fresh testimony of doing things God's way.

CONSTANT GRUMBLING

When you read the story of the children of Israel, you quickly learn they were known for complaining—always murmuring when things were not going right. God delivered them out of Egypt and fed them with manna from heaven, yet they grumbled because there was no water. God instructed Moses to speak to the rock and command water to flow. Now they had water, but it wasn't long before they were unhappy about something else.

The Lord finally brought them to a place where their objective was almost in sight. God told Moses to send twelve men to spy out their promised land. Ten returned saying how bountiful the territory was—flowing with milk and honey. But they began to complain about the size of the giants they saw and how it would be impossible to conquer the land.

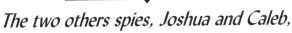

The two others spies, Joshua and Caleb, had an entirely different report. Yes, there were giants, but "we are well able to overtake them."

The doubters and complainers could not visualize the big picture. All they could think of was the problem right in front of them. Scripture records, *"And all the congregation lifted up their voice, and cried; and the people wept that night. And all the children of Israel murmured against Moses and against Aaron: and the whole congregation said unto them, "Would God that we had died in the land of Egypt! Or would God we had died in this wilderness! And wherefore hath the Lord brought us unto this land, to fall by the sword, that our wives and our children should be a prey? Were it not better for us to return into Egypt?"* (Numbers 14:1-3).

Is it any wonder the Almighty became fed up with them?

THE "GOOD OLD DAYS"?

When people become dissatisfied and start complaining, they

often speak of how it used to be, "Well back before I was saved, it seemed like I had more friends than I have now"—or some other comparison. Yes, but you were on your way to hell!

———— ❖ ————

We don't serve a God of the "good old days." He never says He is the great "I was." He proclaims He is the great "I AM."

This means that whatever God has ordained for you, if it was good in the past, it will be better today if you have faith in Him. Therefore, don't allow yourself to think, "Before I started living for God, I had dates all the time. Now that I am saved and trying to live right, it seems like no one is paying any attention to me."

Examine your words. Instead of complaining that there are no good, single men out there, why not start confessing that God has the perfect mate for you.

FORGET THE PAST

Once the children of Israel got into the murmur-and-complain mode, the only thing they could do was reminisce about how it used to be:

And they said one to another, 'Let us make a captain, and let us return into Egypt.' Then Moses and Aaron fell on their faces before all the assembly of the congregation of the children of Israel. And Joshua the son of Nun, and Caleb the son of Jephunneh, which were of them that searched the land, rent their clothes: And they spake unto all the company of the children of Israel, saying, The land, which we passed through to search it, is an exceeding good land. If the Lord delight in us, then He will bring us into this land, and give it us; a land which floweth with milk and honey. Only rebel not against the Lord, neither fear ye the people of the land; for they are bread for us: their defence is departed from them, and the Lord is with us: fear them not.

But all the congregation bade stone them with stones. And the glory of the Lord appeared in the tabernacle of the congregation before all the children of Israel (Numbers 14:4-10).

God was ready to wipe them out, but Moses began to intercede on their behalf. The Lord heard his prayer and said, *"I have pardoned according to thy word: But as truly as I live, all the earth shall be filled with the glory of the Lord. Because all those men which have seen my glory, and my miracles, which I did in Egypt and in the wilderness, and have tempted me now these ten times, and have not hearkened to my voice"* (verses 20-22).

DOUBTING LED TO DEATH

Murmuring, however, can become a habit. It is not something that a person does one time and automatically quits. In the case of the children of Israel, it kept them from entering the Promised Land. As the Bible records:

Surely they shall not see the land which I sware unto their fathers, neither shall any of them that provoked me see it: But my servant Caleb, because he had another spirit with him, and hath followed me fully, him will I bring into the land whereinto he went; and his seed shall possess it (verses 23-24).

And the Lord spake unto Moses and unto Aaron, saying,

*how long shall I bear with this evil congregation, which
murmur against me? I have heard the murmurings of the
children of Israel, which they murmur against me. Say unto
them, As truly as I live, saith the Lord as ye have spoken in
mine ears, so will I do to you: Your carcasses shall fall in this
wilderness; and all that were numbered of you, according to
your whole number, from twenty years old and upward,
which have murmured against me.*

*Doubtless ye shall not come into the land, concerning
which I sware to make you dwell therein, save Caleb the son
of Jephunneh, and Joshua the son of Nun. But your little
ones, which ye said should be a prey, them will I bring in,
and they shall know the land which ye have despised. But as
for you, your carcases, they shall fall in this wilderness. And
your children shall wander in the wilderness forty years, and
bear your whoredoms, until your carcases be wasted in the
wilderness. After the number of the days in which ye
searched the land, even forty days, each day for a year shall
ye bear your iniquities, even forty years, and ye shall know
my breach of promise"* (verses 26-34).

Their murmuring spirit caused the children of Israel to stop in
their tracks. It took forty years to make a journey that should have
taken less than forty days.

Why so long? Because those who doubted God and complained
had to die in the wilderness so He could take a new generation of
young people into the land of promise.

UNUSUAL ORDERS
Personally, I don't want to take the scenic route in life. If it

takes me only six months to get out of debt, I do not want the process to last six years because of the words coming out of my mouth. If it takes me three months for my healing to manifest, I do not want to delay it another three years because of murmuring and complaining.

*I want my words to be of thanks, praise, and worship
—believing that God will do what He has promised.*

If you keep reading the story, Joshua, Caleb and their greatest challenges were still ahead. But now they were a positive, believing band of Israelites ready to defeat any foe.

When it was time to take the city of Jericho, God gave instructions to Joshua. The unusual orders were to have this huge throng of people walk around the city one time daily for the next six days and on the seventh day to walk around the walls of Jericho seven times. After the seventh time, a mighty miracle took place. Here is how Scripture describes what happened:

> *And it came to pass on the seventh day, that they rose early about the dawning of the day, and compassed the city after the same manner seven times: only on that day they compassed the city seven times. And it came to pass at the seventh time, when the priest blew with the trumpets, Joshua said unto the people, Shout; for the Lord has given you the city (Joshua 6:15-16).*
>
> *So the people shouted when the priests blew with the trumpets: and it came to pass, when the people heard the sound of the trumpet, and the people shouted with a great*

*shout, that the wall fell down flat, so that the people went
up into the city, every man straight before him, and they
took the city* (verse 20).

What an awesome sight that must have been!

FROM SILENCE TO SHOUTING

Today, I believe the Lord has cities He wants you to take back.
It's restoration time! We need to shout with the voice of triumph
and victory until it rattles the walls of the devil and causes every
stronghold to come tumbling down.

The reason the younger generation of the children of Israel had
an anointing powerful enough to shout down the walls is because
they were far different than their parents and grandparents in the
wilderness. Instead of complaining they were totally obedient to the
instructions God gave to Joshua.

The Word tells us, *"And Joshua had commanded the people,
saying, Ye shall not shout, nor make any noise with your voice,
neither shall any word proceed out of your mouth, until the day I bid
you shout; then shall ye shout"* (Joshua 6:10).

I am amazed every time I read this account. Biblical historians
calculate there were between one and three million Jews in the
wilderness—and with their offspring that number was multiplied.
Even after the deaths in the desert, Joshua gave a command to a
countless army of people and told them they were getting ready to
march around the city of Jericho the next day. There was no way he
had time to tell each person individually the complete plan. All the
people could do was to start obeying God.

One thing they knew. Joshua passed the word that no one in the camp was to open their mouth and say anything until they were instructed to.

I have difficulty imagining that happening in the church today. "What did you say? Pastor Joshua told me to be quiet? No one tells me what to do. Who does he think he is?"

And I can hear another saying, "Bless God, if we were going to walk around this city, the pastor could have told me this two months ago; I could have had time to buy me some walking shoes. I had a doctor's appointment scheduled for Thursday and now he calls and tells us to walk around the city!"

I am convinced the reason many today are still sick, tired, broke, depressed and discouraged is because they refuse to follow God's instructions.

CLAIMING THE PROMISE

On day one in Jericho they walked around the walls with voices silent, nothing happened. Days two, three, and four were the same. About this time I'm sure somebody considered complaining—until they thought about their forefathers and how their grumbling caused them to be trapped in the wilderness.

Finally, on the seventh march of the seventh day, Joshua gave the signal! Suddenly, in one accord, they lifted their voices and shouted to the Lord. The walls collapsed and they marched in to claim their promise.

A WORD FROM ABOVE

At this very moment, the Lord wants to return things into our hands. Perhaps you are working for an employer who you feel is incompetent. God may be allowing you to stay in that situation so your flesh can be tamed and crucified. He is trying to tell you it is "not by might, nor by power, but it is by my Spirit saith the Lord."

God is giving you a word to sit there and be quiet. Just walk around that wall. Even if you do not understand why you have to keep marching or why you aren't to speak up, if you know you have a directive from the Lord, just do it!

There will come a day when the Almighty will say "It is time to shout!" If you have obeyed Him, without murmuring, complaining, or fault finding, when you open your mouth and shout, there will be unbelievable power. The walls in your life will come tumbling down!

As believers, we must learn how to let the Spirit of God tame our tongues. If you find yourself saying something about an individual or a situation you know in your heart is wrong, quickly repent. Don't allow anything to come between you and God's anointing.

I've seen people who have shouted a great shout, danced a great dance, praised with a great praise, yet nothing happened. Could it be that before they shouted, danced, or praised, their negative vocabulary cut off the power?

I pray that the words of your mouth and the meditation of your heart will be acceptable in God's sight.

EIGHT

COURAGE: YOUR KEY TO CHANGE

There was a time when the currents of life were pulling me in the wrong direction. I had one foot in the world, and the other in church. The Lord started dealing with me and letting me know that I could not continue this half-way life.

He told me I could not have a Sunday morning face and then a rest-of-the-week face. I had to decide that I was not going to anymore parties or continue to hang out with the same crowd. No more drinking, smoking, and messing around. However, I found out my friends didn't mind if I went to church on Sunday as long as I was going to "party" the rest of the week.

After straddling the fence, I told myself if I was going to live this life for Christ, I had to commit to it one hundred and twenty-five percent. When I made that decision, my so-called friends abandoned me. My phone was not ringing off the hook, and I was no longer being invited to go the places I once frequented.

I finally made up my mind that if I didn't have anyone else to hang out with, it would be me, Jesus, the Father God, The Holy Ghost, and the angels of heaven. I was through being a part-time lover to the Lord.

It took a great deal of resolve for me to make this decision, but when I did, I began to hear from the Lord. This is when God literally "commanded" me to leave my job and enroll in Bible school.

"BE NOT AFRAID"

When it was time for Joshua to replace Moses as the leader of the Children of Israel, the Almighty let him know it was going to take courage:

Every place that the sole of your foot shall tread upon, that have I given unto you, as I said unto Moses. From the wilderness and this Lebanon even unto the great river, the river Euphrates, all the land of the Hittites, and unto the great sea toward the going down of the sun, shall be your coast. There shall not any man be able to stand before thee all the days of thy life: as I was with Moses, so I will be with thee: I will not fail thee, nor forsake thee.

Be strong and of a good courage: for unto this people shalt thou divide for an inheritance the land, which I sware unto their fathers to give them. Only be thou strong and very courageous, that thou mayest observe to do according to all the law, which Moses my servant commanded thee: turn not from it to the right hand or to the left, that thou mayest prosper withersoever thou goest.

This book of the law shall not depart out of thy mouth; but thou shalt meditate therein day and night that thou mayest observe to do according to all that is written therein: for then thou shalt make thy way prosperous, and then thou shalt have good success.

*Have not I commanded thee? Be strong and of a good
courage; be not afraid, neither be thou dismayed: for the
Lord thy God is with thee whithersoever thou goest* (Joshua
1:3-9).

IT'S YOUR TERRITORY

Like Joshua, according to the Word, the ground you walk on has
been given to you. God wants you to know that He has more
territory with your name written on it, and great triumphs He is
expecting you to achieve.

It is time for you to proclaim, "I am a dominator. I declare that
God's anointing abides upon me to overcome and conquer every
obstacle that Satan tries to put in front of me."

———— ❖ ————

*You were born to walk in victory from the day
the Creator placed you on this planet.*

In the verses above, God was talking to Joshua, but the Lord is
not a respecter of persons. This means every place that the sole of
your feet walks upon, the Almighty promises He will give it to you.

Within a span of four verses, at three different times God told
Joshua to be strong and courageous—that He had something
special to give him. But in order to possess it, he could not be a
wimp!

To access and have the perfect will of God, you to have to walk
in everything the blood of Jesus has already paid for you. This
requires courage.

NO EXCUSES

I think the Lord was trying to send a message to Joshua because he had taken the reins from the most outstanding leader that Israel had ever known up to that time. When Moses was on the scene, he was used by God to deliver Israel out of Egyptian bondage. The children of Israel saw the Great Jehovah use Moses to part the Red Sea. Remember, when they were hungry, Moses prayed and God rained down manna from the sky. When they were thirsty, Moses struck the rock and it brought forth water. God led them by a pillar of fire by night and a cloud by day. By the time they left Egypt, the Bible tells us they had plenty of silver and gold and there was not one feeble person among them. In other words, they had a mass healing and received supernatural restoration of their wealth.

How would you like to follow a leader who performed such amazing miracles at God's command? Joshua didn't have an easy assignment.

You know how people can be when they are used to one person doing things a particular way. Resisting change, they may comment, "This is not the way so and so said to do it." When people get used to one type of leadership, they are reluctant to change.

For this reason, God began to tell Joshua that if he was going to conquer everything he would need to be very courageous. He didn't need to be timid or make excuses for his speaking or leadership skills. If he expected to walk in what God had ordained for his life, there could be no moaning, groaning, crying, or complaining. It was going to require boldness and inner strength—and total dependence on the Lord.

God is saying the same thing to you today. If you truly expect that every place your feet tread will be yours, there can be no fear, intimidation, or confessing what you *can't* do.

BOLD AS A LION

It's tough to step out in faith when your carnal man has been operating one way for a long period of time. Your flesh wants to resist, but your spirit man is leaping within you, saying, "Yes! Pride, fear, and jealousy—get out of the way!"

The easy way out is to revert back and continue your old habits and behavior. However God's way requires courage—the key to change. As Scripture states, *"The wicked flee when no man pursueth: but the righteous are bold as a lion"* (Proverbs 28:1).

Often, when people are not living right, they think everyone is out to get them. They're always looking over their shoulder, second-guessing motives, interpreting actions falsely, and endeavoring to figure out what is going on.

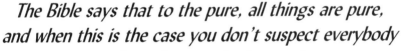

The Bible says that to the pure, all things are pure, and when this is the case you don't suspect everybody around you has an ulterior motive.

The righteous understand who they are in Christ Jesus and refuse to back down when a challenge comes their way. They do not turn around, tuck tail, and run when things get tough. They stand up and are willing to look the devil square in the face and let him know that he is not going to walk in and take their family, their marriage, their children, and their health. In fact, the righteous will become bold and declare, "Devil, if you enter my house, I want you to know that you'll have a fight on your hands."

109

Yes, they are as fearless as a lion! They understand it takes boldness to step out and obey God.

FIGHT THE CURRENT

In our culture, obeying the Lord is not the popular or politically correct path to take. Most people think they live in a "Burger King®️ Society" where you can "have it your way."

Thank God there is liberty in Christ Jesus, but the Lord has some specific rules we must follow. It takes courage to obey His will, to stand and declare you are going to do things God's way, regardless of your surroundings.

It doesn't take any effort to blindly follow the crowd. It's like jumping into a stream and heading down the river. You certainly don't have to fight to flow in the direction of the current—it will carry you downstream. The test comes when you know your destination is in the other direction, upstream.

Today, God is asking you to resist the pull of the world and make some important changes. Do you have the courage He requires?

NINE

SAVED FROM YOURSELF

F ar too many believers are spiritual cowards. They will stand to their feet and praise God when they are surrounded by other Christians. But what happens when the arrows start to fly? How do they react when their associates at work think they are foolish for living by godly principles. What is their response when unsaved relatives accuse them of being part of a cult because they are in church every time the doors open and have stopped smoking and no longer hang out at the bars?

The born again Christian needs to stand and declare to each person who is talking about them, "For God I live, and for God I am willing to die."

It takes courage and conviction to live this life the right way. For instance, fortitude is needed when a man is enticed by a woman who is not his wife. With boldness he needs to look her right in the eyes and say, "I am committed to my wife and my wife only."

God is looking for men and women who will have enough audacity to be strong and do things His way.

It is time for the world to finally see a church that is really living what it preaches. For too long people have used the excuse that everyone in the sanctuary is a hypocrite. But this is no reason for a person to sit at home—especially since there are phonies in every walk of life.

However, the world should be able to see Christians demonstrate what it is to be true followers of Christ. What if your unsaved friend is standing in line behind you at the grocery store and you are about to buy a six pack of Budweiser®? What kind of witness would that be?

You *can* have the strength to live a separated life. Ephesians 3:11-12 reads, *"According to the eternal purpose which He purposed in Christ Jesus our Lord: In whom we have boldness and access with confidence by the faith of Him."*

Only through God's Son can we have such boldness and trust. The Amplified Version says, *"This is in accordance with the terms of the eternal and timeless purpose which He has realized and carried into effect in [the person of] Christ Jesus our Lord, in whom because of our faith in Him, we dare to have the boldness (courage and confidence) of free access (an unreserved approach to God with freedom and without fear)."*

NO MORE GUILT TRIPS

It is vital to know that God will never heap guilt and condemnation on you. The Bible teaches that Satan is the accuser of the brethren. He is the one who sits on your shoulder, always trying to remind you of the mistakes you made in the past. Those accusations are not from God because the Lord never uses remorse to teach us truth.

This is why we should not try to put anyone on a guilt trip. Christians know what behavior they need to shun. Sometimes the Holy Spirit will come along and minister to you, shining the light of the Word in areas you may not have yet thought about. You don't

112

need anyone to preach sin in order for you to make changes. Instead we need to hear, accept, and practice righteousness.

———— ❖ ————

From a pastor's point of view, instead of preaching warnings about what an individual needs to <u>stop</u> doing, I believe we should teach who that person is in Christ Jesus.

DOMINION OVER SIN

In my early years, I attended a church where the preacher yelled and screamed every week, telling me all of the things that I needed to quit doing. I would sit in the pew feeling guilty and condemned. Then, at the end of the service, I would go to the altar and cry my eyes out.

Here's the problem. When we are moved by emotion alone those feelings are temporary and quickly wear off. I hate to admit it, but some Sunday nights when I arrived home and my tears were dry, the phone would ring and I'd be back at the club with my friends.

Nevertheless, I would feel guilty and cry again the following Sunday.

As time passed, I desired to find out who I was in Christ Jesus. Someone sat down with me and taught me that I was not born to live a life of confusion. In those sessions, there was no yelling or shouting; instead, I was led to open the Bible and read the Word for myself. I began to learn that from the creation of this world, I was ordained to be just like God since I was born in His image. I found out what a privilege it is to be called a son of the Most High.

When I realized I was made the righteousness of God in Christ Jesus, I decided on my own accord that I was not going back to the nightclub scene anymore—it was no longer worthy of my presence. I decided that I was not going to drink again because my body is the temple of the Holy Ghost.

Once I found out that I had dominion over iniquity and no longer needed to sin, I made a decision that I was not going to remain in that lifestyle any longer. Don't get me wrong. There were times I missed the mark, but I eventually reached the place where I hit the target far more than falling short.

This did not happen because of guilt and condemnation, rather because the Word of God brought conviction to my heart. A man or woman who truly loves the Lord will not do anything to hurt his loving heavenly Father.

THE FALLEN ANGEL

Do you know what Satan hates more than anything else in his life? He despises the fact that he made one great mistake.

One day, in a fit of pride, the devil became arrogant and lifted himself up, confessed that he was going to ascend above the heights of the clouds, above the stars, and be like the Most High. When he did, God cast Lucifer down to the ground. He became a fallen angel and has never had a chance to repent. All of the other angels that followed him were kicked out of heaven as well and became demonic spirits—and remained that way.

You and I, on the other hand, have a long list of errors we have made. If we each opened the pages of the history book which records our past, the chronicle of things we have done wrong would be long indeed. We have all sinned against God in different ways.

Then someone comes along and ministers the Good News of Jesus. We accept Christ into our heart, confess Him as our Lord, and believe that God has raised Him from the dead. The Father takes the blood of His Son, wipes all our sins away, and gives us a brand new start. He makes us a new creation—as if we have never sinned at any time in our lives.

Although we know this truth, there are still times when we fall short. Have you missed the mark since being saved? Some of us need to lift *both* hands!

GET BACK UP!

Now comes the part Satan cannot stand. As believers, if we get off track, then return to God and sincerely repent, the Lord still wipes the sin away through the blood of Jesus Christ and treats us as if He never saw the transgression.

It takes courage to get up after you have fallen. Sometimes when you are feeling bad, you feel justified to remain in your sin, and even wallow in it. But let me share this secret: you don't get any bonus points in heaven for sitting around feeling sorry for yourself after you have messed up.

———— ❖ ————

Rise up, repent before God, and believe
by faith that you are forgiven.

This not only refers to when you have blown it by making a mistake; it also includes the times you know what God told you to do, and still disobeyed.

The blood of Jesus gives us authority to be able to approach God and say, "Lord, I repent. Whatever is in me that has caused me to sin against You, I ask your forgiveness, and Lord, save me from me."

Then stand to your feet, march yourself back to the house of

115

God, lift up holy hands, and worship the Lord as if you have never sinned a day in your life.

BEWARE OF THE TESTS

You should know by now that every time you have a major triumph, be on guard. If you get a new promotion, watch out. By no means am I saying to be frightened or intimidated because the Bible tells us to be sober and vigilant (1 Peter 5:8). In other words, pay attention.

———— ❖ ————

Don't become so caught up in celebrating that you forget the fact that the enemy will do his best to attack you during your time of rejoicing.

A word of warning. If God prophecies something wonderful over your life, rest assured the devil will start plotting. If the Lord tells you that you are about to be blessed financially, you'll probably have an unexpected bill show up first. This is not a negative confession, but something I have seen happen.

The Bible teaches that tribulations, persecutions, and afflictions come for the Word's sake (Mark 4:17). As soon as you step into manifestation you begin to walk into a greater level of understanding of Scripture. Then the enemy will appear and tempt you to see what you are really made of. He will try to find out if you are going to stand with God and do it His way, or turn around, retreat, and give in.

I pray that is such a test you will emerge from the fire as pure gold.

Never be discouraged. What the Lord promises, He fulfills.

BE CAREFUL WHAT YOU SEE

There is an important lesson to be learned from what happened in the life of David. Scripture records, *"And it came to pass, after the year was expired, at the time when kings go forth to battle, that David sent Joab, and his servants with him, and all Israel; and they destroyed the children of Ammon, and besieged Rabbah. But David tarried still at Jerusalem"* (2 Samuel 11:1).

Then we read, *"And it came to pass in an evening tide, that David arose from off his bed, and walked upon the roof of the king's house: and from the roof he saw a woman washing herself; and the woman was very beautiful to look upon"* (verse 2).

David let his eyes get the best of him. He allowed himself to view something that he had no business looking at. When men and women permit themselves to see things that can cause a potential downfall, it is eventually going to harm them. This is true whether you are single or married. You may say, "I just watch those pornographic videos to help put me in the mood. I'm married, so it really doesn't matter."

Even if you are husband and wife, you still have to keep a watch on your sexual appetite? Sex is like a drug. If you let it go unchecked you will reach the place where even the confines of your marriage union will not be enough to satisfy. Before you know it, if you continue watching what you have no business viewing, you will be expecting your spouse to engage in the same activities you saw in those movies. You will soon find yourself frustrated, maybe even growing unhappy with your wife's appearance, and with her sexually. Why? Because other women have been in front of your eyes—and all of a sudden you no longer see your wife the way you used to. If you do not control this, you will find yourself looking for

117

someone else who mirrors what you have seen in the movies. It is a demonic trick of the enemy.

WHY ISN'T IT WORKING?

Single people also need to understand the necessity of taming their flesh before they get married. I know the Bible says that it is better to marry than to burn [with passion] (2 Corinthians 7:9), but it is even better to commit your human urges to the Lord before you are married—to get your flesh under control.

Don't just jump up and marry anyone because your emotions are running wild. There are too many people rushing to the marriage altar just because they want to be able to have sex. I have news for you. If you don't have anything in your marriage other than sex, you will be singing "The thrill is gone" in a big hurry.

———— ❖ ————

It takes more than just two bodies coming together to make a true marriage.

Far too many skip the premarital counseling process and dash to the courthouse for someone to give them a quick fix. Sadly, millions of couples are taught nothing about marriage prior to the ceremony and then they wonder why it is not working. They are getting married for the wrong reasons.

With God's help, tame your flesh and get your body under control first.

A WICKED PLAN

Let's turn back to the king's rooftop where David saw a gorgeous woman washing herself. The Bible tells us, *"David sent and inquired after the woman. And one said, Is not this Bath-sheba, the daughter of Eliam, the wife of Uriah the Hittite? And David sent messengers, and took her; and she came in unto him, and he lay with her; for she was purified from her uncleanness: and she returned unto her house. And the woman conceived, and sent and told David, and said, I am with child"* (2 Samuel 11:3-5).

Think of it! David slept with a woman who was another man's wife. To make matters worse, the natural process had taken over and she became pregnant. David knew he had a problem on his hands, so he sent for Bathsheba's husband, Uriah, who was out fighting in a battle. The idea was for the man to lay down with his wife, thinking he could trick Uriah into believing the child she was carrying was his.

The husband was such an honorable person regarding his commitment to battle, that when he returned to the city, he would not even go home. Instead, he slept at the door of David's house. After several unsuccessful attempts to entice Uriah to meet with his wife, David devised a second plan. He ordered that the army send a unit that included Uriah into the fiercest field of combat—then retreat and leave him to be killed in battle.

This wicked plan worked (verses 15-17).

FACE TO FACE WITH SIN

When Bathsheba heard Uriah was dead, Scripture records:

She mourned for her husband. And when the mourning was past, David sent and fetched her to his house, and she became his wife, and bare him a son. But the thing that David had done displeased the Lord (2 Samuel 11:26-27).

And the Lord sent Nathan unto David. And he came

unto him, and said unto him, There were two men in one city; the one rich and the other poor. The rich man had exceeding many flocks and herds: But the poor man had nothing, save one little ewe lamb, which he had bought and nourished up: and it grew up together with him, and with his children; it did eat of his own meat, and drank of his own cup, and lay in his bosom, and was unto him as a daughter. And there came a traveller unto the rich man, and he spared to take of his own flock and of his own herd, to dress for the wayfaring man that was come unto him; but took the poor man's lamb, and dressed it for the man that was to come to him.

And David's anger was greatly kindled against the man; and he said to Nathan, As the Lord liveth, the man that hath done this thing shall surely die: And he shall restore the lamb fourfold, because he did this thing, and because he had no pity. And Nathan said to David, Thou art the man" (1 Samuel 12:1-7).

David said unto Nathan, I have sinned against the Lord. And Nathan said unto David, The Lord hath put away thy sin; thou shalt not die. Howbeit, because by this deed thou hast given great occasion to the enemies of the Lord to blaspheme, the child also that is born unto thee shall surely die (verses 13-14).

We can see how David opened up the door for the enemy to attack this child. The story continues: *But when David saw that his servants whispered, David perceived that the child was dead: therefore David said unto his servants, Is the child dead? And they said, he is dead. Then David arose from the earth, and washed, and anointed himself, and changed his apparel, and came into the house of the Lord, and worshipped: then he came to his own house; and when he required, they set bread before him, and he did eat* (verses 19-20).

David recognized that he had sinned and had missed the mark, yet he did not run away from God. He had enough sense to return to the temple and repent. This is why the Lord called David, *"A man after mine own heart"* (Acts 13:22).

Following this heart-wrenching episode, David was once more used mightily by God.

THE TURN-AROUND

If you should ever fall or make a major mistake, open your Bible and read this account again. Like David, turn around and run back home to your heavenly Father as fast as you can. Fall to your knees and admit your failings and the fact that you have disobeyed God's instructions. You'll find that His forgiveness will rain down on you because the Lord *"is rich in mercy"* (Ephesians 2:4). Plus, *"his mercy is everlasting; and his truth endureth to all generations"* (Psalm 100:5).

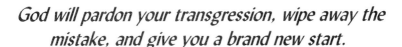

God will pardon your transgression, wipe away the mistake, and give you a brand new start.

Don't turn to the Lord simply because you were caught. Rather, you must be willing to do what David did and change your behavior. But never forget that forgiveness is available to you. Even though you may have broken the fellowship, you are still God's child and He loves you as His own.

THE PROVISION OF PARDON

We have to understand the depth of the blood of Jesus. Do you think God is going to let us slip away from Him for making one mistake? If it were going to be that easy, you can be sure that the Father would not have allowed His only Son to go through the trials of life and death itself on our behalf. God has made provision so when you stumble after salvation, there is forgiveness available.

This makes me want to shout, "Hallelujah!"

I rejoice that I can lift up my hands and know God loves me and will pardon me. As Scripture declares, *"For we have not a high priest which cannot be touched with the feeling of our infirmities; but was in all points tempted like as we are, yet without sin. Let us therefore come boldly (courageously and with confidence) unto the throne of grace, that we may obtain mercy, and find grace to help in time of need"* (Hebrews 4:15).

In other words Jesus understands the temptations of the flesh.

———— ❖ ————

When God cleans you up, don't come
tip-toeing back into His presence.

Once you have repented, return with your chest out and your head held high, expecting the Lord to bless your life just as He did before you made a wrong turn. Come believing that He will restore you and pour blessings over you exactly as He has done in the past.

People may try to convince you that you don't deserve the favor God is bestowing. Tell them, "I'm glad the Lord's grace is not based on whether you think I am worthy."

According to the Word, you are worthy (Revelation 3:4)! You can enter once more into His presence.

KEEP PRESSING IN

If you listen to some people's version of the subject, they will make you think that repentance means you need to sit around in sackcloth and ashes with a sad face. In God's sight, however, it's a matter of the heart.

Should you commit a transgression, don't let one minute pass before you recognize your mistake and turn to the Lord. Go to Him with a contrite heart and a determination you will never walk that path again.

Be like the woman who persevered until Jesus heard her plea:

> *Behold, a woman of Canaan...cried unto Him, saying, Have mercy on me, O Lord, thou son of David; my daughter is grievously vexed with a devil. But he answered her not a word. And his disciples came and besought him, saying, Send her away; for she crieth after us. But He answered and said, I am not sent but unto the lost sheep of the house of Israel.*
>
> *Then came she and worshipped Him saying, Lord help me. But He answered and said, It is not meet to take the children's bread, and to cast it to the dogs. And she said, Truth, Lord: yet the dogs eat of the crumbs which fall from their masters' table. Then Jesus answered and said unto her, O woman, great is thy faith: be it unto thee even as thou wilt. And her daughter was made whole from that very hour* (Matthew 15:22-28).

Yes, there are times you feel like quitting and your flesh says, "That is enough!" But to receive what God has for you, push beyond your emotions.

IS THIS YOUR DAY?

Perhaps you have been standing in faith regarding a matter for a long time and it has not manifested—yet you are still confessing the Word and rejoicing in advance. Don't stop, no matter what anyone tells you. Keep pushing on and never allow your feelings to get the best of you. To be specific, it takes courage to go home to a spouse who does not know how to treat you. Keep on pressing into God because if He promised to bring the answer, He will!

Even if things look hopeless at the moment, have confidence and know that the Lord is working it out.

It may not happen by the end of the night or the week, but declare this is your year and that you will see God perform His Word.

This principle can be applied to every aspect of your life. For example, you may be a single adult looking for a mate and wanting God to send you the right person. While you wait you will likely be approached by attractive, unsaved people. But you know what the Scripture says regarding being unequally yoked (2 Corinthians 6:14).

It is easy to give up and say, "Forget it! I'll go ahead and get married and pray God can save him (or her) once we tie the knot."

Don't fall for this trap of Satan. Instead, stand on the Word and wake up tomorrow proclaiming, "I believe this is the day the Lord will answer my prayer and come through for me."

When I believe God for something and it doesn't show up, I am determined to rise the next morning and say, "Yes, this is probably the day for manifestation." When I do, I am speaking the word of faith—and you should too.

PROVE GOD NOW!

It also takes fortitude and commitment to tithe and honor God with your substance, even though your checkbook says you cannot afford it. We can't trust in ourselves, looking at our bank balance and waiting until we get to a place where we have enough to give the Lord the "tenth" that is rightfully His.

As long as you are waiting for conditions to change, you will never begin. There will always be some emergency that shows up to keep you from doing what God commands.

The Bible is clear regarding this matter:

Will a man rob God? Yet ye have robbed me. But ye say, wherein have we robbed thee? In tithes and offerings. Ye are cursed with a curse: for ye have robbed me, even this whole nation. Bring ye all the tithes into the storehouse, that there may be meat in mine house, and prove me now herewith saith the Lord of hosts, if I will not open you the windows of heaven, and pour you out a blessing, that there shall not be room enough to receive it. And I will rebuke the devourer for your sakes, and he shall not destroy the fruits of your ground; neither shall your vine cast her fruit before the time in the field, saith the Lord of hosts. And the nations shall call you blessed for you shall be a delightsome land" (Malachi 3:8-12).

We must reach a point where we have enough courage to prove God now! He did not say prove Him next week or next month. The

Lord declared, *"prove me now"* to see if He would open heaven's windows and pour out a super-abundant blessing.

Are you willing to put God to the test?

Declare that you will never be broke another day in your life. Look the devil in the eye and tell him this is your year of increase and restoration—that you will get everything back.

It's not only necessary to be saved from our sin, but we must be saved from ourselves—from our doubts and fears.

This is your year for joy, peace, anointing, health, wealth, and to receive every blessing God has for you! Declare you have it now; that Satan has to give up what is rightfully yours. Let your spirit speak your destiny and declare victory!

TEN

THE RESULTS OF CHANGE

God does not ask us to make adjustments erratically or for no reason. Anytime the Lord ministers a word concerning casting off old ways of thinking and long-held attitudes, He is preparing us for the divine favor He desires to place on our lives. In the process, God will begin to equip us with His way of thinking. He has blessings with your name on them!

Since the Lord knows the end from the beginning, in order for you to walk in everything He has pre-arranged on your pathway of victory, there are some corrective measures to be made. Once you make these changes, you become qualified to step up to the next level of His blessings.

We all are at different stages of our journey. Some are filled to overflowing with God's oil of anointing, while others are just getting started. Please know that the Lord showers us with His goodness as much as He can considering what He has to work with!

God will always bless us to our maximum capacity. Prior to reading this book, spiritually, your ability may have been the size of a coffee cup, but the Lord has filled it as much as He can. No matter how much more praying, fasting or believing God you do He could not pour any more into that cup than you had room to receive.

The Lord has been talking to us concerning pride, arrogance, getting over fear of rejection, conquering jealousy, envy, backbiting, murmuring, complaining, and rebelling against authority. Guess what has happened? When you started to make those adjustments, what you literally did in the spirit realm was to step up to the snack bar of heaven. You have traded in that coffee cup and told Him you are now ready for a big pitcher. Praise God! And some of you have stepped out and traded up to the size of a bathtub!

If you have more room to receive, God knows how to fill it to the brim! And now that you have started making corrections you should expect new manifestations.

In Third John 2 we read, *"Beloved, I wish above all things (that word "all" literally means in all things or concerning all things) that thou mayest prosper and be in health, even as thou soul prospereth."*

TOTAL RESTORATION

Our heavenly Father desires for us to experience success in every part of our lives. Many gain a measure of prosperity in three, four, or five areas, but wherever you are still lacking, the Lord wants those to be flourishing as well.

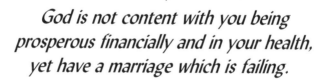

God is not content with you being prosperous financially and in your health, yet have a marriage which is failing.

I believe this is a time of total restoration when the Lord is going to connect you with some individuals you have not spoken to in years. He is going to repair relationships where mothers and fathers may have written you off, or you may have distanced yourself from them because of some conflict that happened in the past. I believe this is the year people are going to come in contact with relatives they have been separated from for a long time.

Since you have done some required fine-tuning, God is now ready to release the floodgates and bring people back into your life because your "love walk" is now strong enough to overcome their lack of affection for you.

The Scripture says "I wish above *all* things"—which means the sky's the limit. It is up to us how far we want to go. If we maintain a bad attitude, a lifestyle of procrastination, and a lack of organization, then we are saying that we are going to keep our little coffee cups and prosper only to that level. But when you open up your heart, and cry, "Lord, save me from me! Show me things on the inside that need to be corrected," our very soul begins to prosper.

As we learn how to become more submissive to God and not allow our emotions to dominate, but instead permit our spirit to dictate our actions, we position ourselves for prosperity—and much more.

RULES OF THE ROAD

Since gaining a greater wisdom in this area, I am at the altar continually searching my own heart. The Bible says, *"Now these are the commandments, statutes, and the judgment, which the Lord your God command to teach you, that ye might do them in the land wither you go to possess it"* (Deuteronomy 6:1).

Just like the children of Israel, God has a Promised Land awaiting you. But there are rules you must obey as you prepare for the journey to your new territory.

What the Lord has been teaching us is not for us to just hear, nod our heads, say how good it sounds, then do nothing:

- If God has been dealing with you concerning walking in greater forgiveness, then find someone who you need to extend the hand of forgiveness to.

- If you believe God for deliverance, ask Him to show you how to receive deliverance and walk in it.

- If you know you have a bad attitude toward authority, then ask the Lord to help you in the area of submission.

Let me give you an example. When you see a sign on the highway that reads "65 MPH," are you adhering to the speed limit? To do otherwise is a form of rebellion against authority. When you are in the grocery store and you get in the line with the sign that reads "10 Items or Less" and you know you have seventeen items in your basket, getting in that line is a form of rebelling against authority. God is not willing to lift you to the next level if you are still limping from what you have been dealing with in your present state.

BIG TIME BLESSINGS!

The Word tells us what we can expect when we obey His requirements:

Thou mightest fear the Lord God, to keep all his statues and his commandments, which I command thee, thou, and thy son, and thy son's son, all the days of thy life; and that thy days may be prolonged. Hear therefore, O Israel, and observe to do it; (In other words as soon as you begin to do it, this is what happens) that it may be well with thee, and that ye may increase mightily, as the Lord God of thy fathers hath promised thee, in the land that floweth with milk and honey" (Deuteronomy 6:2-3).

To move forward we must observe and pay attention to what we have been taught. God is not interested in just giving you a small-scale increase. With Him, "a little dab will not do you." He wants to bless you BIG time. He is a God that can take you from a "thousand status" to a "millionaire status."

———— ❖ ————

The Lord is not only concerned about you, but He has your children, grandchildren, and great-grandchildren on His mind.

He is trying to use you to birth generational blessings into your family life.

Once you learn God's principles and teach them to your children and your children's children, they will be a part of your family legacy from now on—and your offspring will not have to wrestle with the things you have struggled with. We have to love our families enough to say, "I will surrender my own flesh to the Lord so the rest of my generation will be blessed mightily."

PREPARE FOR AN OVERFLOW

Speaking personally, every single area of my life has increased greatly since I began applying the Word of God. When you make the necessary changes, it does not take the Almighty forever to move you into your Promised Land. My marriage and my family have been blessed; my health has prospered, and yours will too.

There was a chapter in my life when every year around the same time, I would have cold or flu symptoms, and my wife used to constantly get sinus infections. We lived our lives like so many —with a medicine cabinet full of practically everything the pharmacy sold.

As soon as symptoms would show up, we would start medicating. However, we finally reached the place where we started speaking the Word more frequently, letting God make adjustments in our love walk. As I write these words, we are living free of sickness. Our finances have increased mightily. We have gone from living in a small apartment to having a house the Spirit of God directed us to build. We have moved from barely getting by to now experiencing overflow.

NO LACK

Let me remind you that the Almighty is not a respecter of persons.

———— ❖ ————

If you will do what the Spirit has been teaching you, the Lord has a "mighty increase" with your name on it.

In many respects, the church where I grew up had it all wrong. They used to tell us, "God would punish your life by putting sickness on you." But the Lord does not cause illness or infirmity.

Some point to the Scripture which reads, *"Thou shall also consider in thine heart, that, as a man chasteneth his son, so the Lord thy God chasteneth thee"* (Deuteronomy 8:5). However, God does not chasten us with sickness or disease, poverty, calamity, or tragedies. God reproves us by pointing out things that need to be corrected. Yes, sometimes we need to be "spanked" by the Word.

Instead of punishment, if we walk in obedience, there are awesome rewards:

> *Therefore thou shall keep the commandments of the Lord thy God, to walk in His ways, and to fear him. For the Lord thy God bringeth thee into a good land, a land of brooks of water, of fountains and depths that spring out valleys and hills; A land of wheat and barley, and vines, and fig trees, and pomegranates; a land of oil, olive, and honey; A land wherein thou shalt eat bread without scarceness, thou shalt not lack anything in it* (Deuteronomy 8:6-9).

Your heavenly Father is trying to take you somewhere special. He has a place waiting where you will not have to sit around figuring out if you have enough money or whether your body feels good enough to get out of bed and walk. You are headed for a Promised Land, and I am not talking about the "sweet by-and-by"—rather the "sweet right now."

The Lord says if you will just follow Him and obey His commands He is leading you to a good land with your name inscribed on the deed.

THE FORMER AND LATTER RAIN

What happens when you do things God's way? What can you expect to see in your life once you get over that anger, grief, laziness, and lack of timeliness? The Lord promises that He will not only bless you, but keep on pouring out His favor until you are totally restored and satisfied.

133

The showers of heaven are about to start drenching you:

> *Be glad then, ye children of Zion and rejoice in the Lord your God: for he hath given you the former rain moderately, and he will cause to come down for you the rain, the former rain and the latter rain in the first month. And the floors shall be full of wheat, and the fats shall over flow with wine and oil. And I will restore to you the years that the locust hath eaten, the cankerworm, and the caterpillar, and the palmerworm, my great army which I sent among you. And ye shall eat in plenty, and be satisfied, and praise the name of the Lord your God that hath dealt wondrously with you: and my people shall never be ashamed* (Joel 2:23-29).

I love it when God begins to speak to me this way. It is a season of restoration!

IT'S YOUR TIME

Some of you may have lost your home because you were not organized in financial matters. The effects of your previous actions may have caused you to harm your credit, but since the Lord has been teaching you the right way to manage your finances in line with the Word, God is going to restore your credit history. The Almighty can even GIVE you a house supernaturally.

The banks may have told you "no" but the Spirit of God is saying if you do what He has been teaching you to do, He will say a loud "yes" and no one can keep you from receiving what the Lord arranges and provides.

Maybe you once taught or sang with an anointing. Perhaps you used to minister and lay hands on the sick. You may feel like that

LORD, SAVE ME FROM ME!

anointing has left you, but God restores callings and positions, and when you permit yourself to be submitted to Him, He will bring you back to a place of honor.

———— ❖ ————

Now that you have allowed the Lord to save you from yourself, and you are committed to correcting those areas in your life, God will restore ALL because He's in the restoration business!

The psalmist writes, *"Thou shalt arise, and have mercy upon Zion: for the time to favour her, yea the set time, is come"* (Psalms 102:13).

GREATER WORKS

As a result of how the Lord is transforming you, there will be greater manifestations in your life. You may wonder how, but think about it. When you get rid of anger or a poor attitude, people will want to spend more time around you. And when you begin blessing others, they want to be a part of the blessing.

I can attest to this. After I began casting off the negative factors in my life, wisdom and favor began to increase. According to the Word there is a set moment for this to happen, and you need to claim it now. At a certain time, *"Jesus increased in wisdom and stature, and in favour with God and man"* (Luke 2:52).

The Bible teaches us that Christ is our example and the works He did, we should expect to do—and even greater works because He was returning to His Father (John 14:12).

Also, just as we see in the life of Jesus, God wants us to have increased favor with man. Why is this important? Before answering the question, read this verse: *"Give, and it shall be given unto you: good measure, pressed down, shaken together, and running over, shall men give unto your bosom. For with the same measure that you mete withal it shall be measured to you again"* (Luke 6:38).

If you study the context of this particular passage you'll find it's referring to forgiveness. Jesus is saying if you sow forgiveness to someone else, then forgiveness comes back to you. If you give or sow love, then love will return.

––––––––– ❖ –––––––––

The principle of seed time and harvest has
no limitation, and it also pertains to finances.

IS IT GOD?

There may be a need in your life and you don't know where to turn. What you require could be close at hand, but your negative disposition will keep people and blessing from you.

It is essential to maintain a constant check on your attitude. This is why I smile at everybody. I might be in the presence of a billionaire, but if I display a sour demeanor, it could stop him from obeying God and blessing our church.

As a pastor, there are times the Spirit of God will speak to me about giving help to a particular person I don't know well. When this happens I stop, check my own spirit, and make sure it is of the Lord. I want to have peace concerning the matter. Then I talk with my wife to get a confirmation. The reason I go through this long process is to be certain it truly is God speaking.

On the other hand there are some individuals the Lord will ask me to bless, and because I know them so well, I can make the decision almost instantly.

Now let me talk about you—as a potential recipient of God's favor. When you begin to work on what we have discussed in this book you become the kind of person others *want* to share their abundance with. If you have a pleasant disposition instead of walking around with a chip on your shoulder, people will not have a problem blessing you. God's favor will rest so strong on your life that even unbelievers will shower you with unexpected favor.

DON'T ABORT A BLESSING

The Lord has shown me again and again that people are working too hard for "things."

There were times when my wife and I would take money out of our savings or checking account to pay for items we could not afford. In certain instances, God let us know that if we would just slow down and give Him enough time, He had already begun speaking to someone about blessing us with what we were planning to buy.

And just the opposite, the Lord will drop an individual in our hearts and we may not know anything about their particular situation or circumstance. The Spirit of God will tell us to write a check and bless that person.

But what if you don't slow down long enough to hear from the Lord and instead rush out to buy what the Spirit of God has spoken to someone else in regard to your situation. You then abort the blessing of God—and the person the Lord spoke to about giving to you would walk away figuring perhaps they missed it. They think, "Maybe I wasn't supposed to bless them after all."

If you give the Lord a chance, He can bring certain things your way that you won't have to work to receive.

KINGS AND QUEENS

Husbands, if you learn how to become the kind of person who ministers to your wife—one who loves her, talks to her with kindness, sits and listens to her—then you'll discover you will have far more favor with your spouse. When you begin talking to her like she is the queen of your heart, she will in turn treat you like a king.

Your wife doesn't only want to hear sweet words when you are ready to be intimate; it's amazing how romantic our talk becomes then. But what about at other times?

Wives, if you will learn how to respect your man, he will find a way to buy you that new dress, car, or eventually get you into that new home. Show appreciation for what he *has* done and avoid talking about his failures.

When you allow your life to line up with the blessings of God, even within your family, you will have increased favor at home. Those you love will be anxious to do things for you they had not been willing to do in the past.

OPEN YOUR HAND

I confess everyday that I have favor—that it goes before me, follows and surrounds me. As a result, everywhere I go people do great things for me daily. In turn, I am continually looking for ways to reciprocate. I don't walk around with a closed fist, trying to keep everything for myself. I'm much happier when I'm giving.

For instance, I may run into one of the members of the church in the barbershop. If I can get out before they do, I will slip the barber some money to pay for that person's haircut.

This has also happened to me. Someone will see me getting a trim and pay the bill before I can get out of the chair. This is the way it is supposed to be in the Body of Christ. We should always be looking for a way to bless others.

You may be sitting in a restaurant and notice a family across the way who goes to your church. Ask the waiter the cost of their meal and pay for it—and don't forget to leave a generous tip. When you start planting seeds of love, your own favor will multiply.

It's Scriptural. As God told the children of Israel, *"Because they met you not with bread and water in the way, when ye came forth out of Egypt; and because they hired against thee Balaam the son of Beor of Pethor of Mesopotamia, to curse thee. Nevertheless the Lord thy God would not hearken unto Balaam; but the Lord thy God turned the curse into a blessing unto thee, because the Lord thy God loved thee"* (Deuteronomy 23:4-5).

God will turn what is cursed into blessings. You may have been abused by your parents or by your spouse. Perhaps you are suffering with low self-esteem, walking around dejected with your head down, and an inferiority complex, never feeling like you could amount to anything.

------- ❖ -------

Let the Lord perform a
great transformation as only He can.

THE GREAT EXCHANGE

I firmly believe that if God can use me He can use *anybody*. Do not tell me what I can't do, because I know the Lord is on my side. Since this is true, I can accomplish *all* things through Christ who gives me strength.

I may have grown up on the East Side of Detroit, moved from place to place, and been raised by a single parent who did the best she could to bring me up. Statistically, I should be a failure, but I refuse to be, because the Lord is on my side.

God continues to exchange curses for blessings. Everything the devil meant for my detriment, the Lord is turning around. Now I am rising to the top. With God on my side, I will do His will, accomplish great things, and prosper abundantly. I will be blessed in the city, blessed in the field, blessed in the store, blessed coming in and blessed going out, because the Lord is on my side (Deuteronomy 28).

Praise God!

SPEAK TO YOURSELF

The marriage you have struggled with for years may look cursed, but when you begin to act on what God has taught you, He will turn your home into one that is blessed.

To see this accomplished we must obey Him and make the changes He demands. But there is something else He requires of us. It involves speaking to *yourself.*

The prophet Ezekiel wrote:

> *The hand of the Lord was upon me, and carried me out in the spirit of the Lord, and set me down in the midst of the valley which was full of bones. And caused me to pass by them round about: And, behold, there were very many in the open valley; and, lo, they were very dry. And he said unto me, Son of man, can these bones live? And I answered, O Lord God, thou knowest. Again he said unto me prophesy upon these bones and say unto them, O ye dry bones, hear the Word of the Lord.*
>
> *Thus saith the Lord God unto these bones; Behold I will cause breath to enter into you, and ye shall live. And I will*

lay sinews upon you and will bring up flesh upon you, and
cover you with skin, and put breath in you, and ye shall live;
and ye shall know that I am the Lord. So I prophesied as I
was commanded: and as I prophesied, there was a noise, and
behold a shaking, and the bones came together, bone to his
bone (Ezekiel 37:1-7).

This is the same question God has been asking us through this
teaching. "Can this physical body live? Can your family be restored?
Can your checkbook stay alive?"

The Lord is reminding you that you are a "speaking spirit" and
if you are expecting for these dry places in your life to spring to life,
you have to obey Him and begin to talk like you believe it.
Remember what you say determines what you will have.

PROCLAIM IT NOW!

Start prophesying over yourself—and don't be shy, because
shyness is a form of fear. Instead, call yourself bold in the Lord.
Start proclaiming that you *can* do all things through Christ. Declare
your business is blessed, your children are obedient, your husband
is coming into the Kingdom of God, your wife is lining up with the
Word, your family life is in order, and you have more money than
you know what to do with.

Prophesy! Open your mouth and say it! Even when you can't
see the answer, keep proclaiming: "As for me, my house and my
generation, we will serve the Lord."

When God hears you say from the depths of your heart, "Lord,
save me from me!" you can rest assured He will do exactly that.

Your greatest days are just ahead.

141

FOR A COMPLETE LIST OF MEDIA RESOURCES
OR TO SCHEDULE THE AUTHOR FOR
SPEAKING ENGAGEMENTS, CONTACT:

BISHOP GEORGE L. DAVIS
FAITH CHRISTIAN CENTER
8985 LONE STAR ROAD
JACKSONVILLE, FL 32211

PHONE 904-725-3636

EMAIL: vwhitted@fccfl.org
INTERNET: www.georgedavis.org
www. fccjax.com